Hidden Valleys
and
Unknown Shores

Hidden Valleys and Unknown Shores

by

MARIE M. KEESING

illustrated by Charles Robinson

Harcourt Brace Jovanovich

New York and London

First edition

B C D E F G H I J K

Library of Congress Cataloging in Publication Data

Keesing, Marie Margaret Martin.
    Hidden valleys and unknown shores.

    SUMMARY: Two youngsters describe their adventures in
an isolated New Zealand valley where their father
runs an general store.
    [1. New Zealand—Fiction]   I. Robinson, Charles,
1931–   II. Title.
PZ7.K2515Hi   [Fic]   77–88963
ISBN 0–15–232582–4

30018

Contents

ONE   Adrift   3

TWO   Mysterious Mokoia   11

THREE   Paul Disappears   19

FOUR   The Sacrifice   27

FIVE   Green Paint   37

SIX   The Lambeths   43

SEVEN   Paradise Valley   51

EIGHT   We Become Celebrities   59

NINE   The Bull of the Swamps   65

TEN   Big-Game Hunting   77

ELEVEN   "To the Four Kings"   85

TWELVE   Vacation by the Sea   91

THIRTEEN   The Rescue   97

FOURTEEN   The Pony   109

FIFTEEN   The Wild Ride   123

SIXTEEN   Farewell   135

Hidden Valleys
and
Unknown Shores

Adrift

"Let's get into that boat, Eve, and pretend we're going out to the island," said my brother Paul.

On this first sunny day of the long school vacation, adventure was in the air, and the old rowboat tied deep in a clump of willows looked most tempting. We would never, of course, untie it because the river was in flood and the current too strong, and because there were no oars.

"Right, mate!" I cried. "Haul her in." We climbed aboard quickly and let our vessel swing out as far as the rope would allow. It bumped and swung in its restricted arc.

Paul and I had explored most of the pleasant valley near our New Zealand home, but there was one mysterious area that for us symbolized the unknown—yet it lay almost always within our view across Lake Rotorua. It was the island out in the center—Mokoia—a sacred island of the Maori people, the native people of New Zealand. Sometimes we could see smoke rising from the top of its dark green slopes.

We lay down in the bottom of the boat and closed our eyes. It was an old trick of ours, this closing our eyes and taking turns telling what was happening. The game was to leave the other person to take up the tale in the midst of some hair-raising predicament for which an escape had to be invented.

The boat was bumping fiercely in the current, which in our tale became a storm tossing us about in mid-ocean.

"I'm trying to hold onto this wheel," Paul shouted. "Unleash yourself from the bunk, pal. You'll have to come and help. Your turn, Eve."

At that moment we both became aware that our boat was moving at a fast and increasing speed. We sat up so suddenly that it nearly capsized. Paul yelled while I sat dumb with fright. There we were, far out beyond the river mouth, moving into the lake. The boat, swinging in the current, had frayed the rope; our make-believe voyage had become real.

We yelled to "Old Kate," the Maori woman with the tattooed chin who lived with her grandchild in a moss-covered hut on the far side of the river, but she was deaf, so we knew our shouting was hopeless. Some people were strolling along the beach near the timber mill. We waved and screamed to them, but they looked as small as stick figures and did not hear or see us.

"Should we try to swim for it, Eve?"

"Look at the river current," I replied. "It's strong right out to those lake waves where the color of the water changes." Actually neither of us was much good at swimming, and we felt safer in the boat.

"Maybe after we get out of the river current, the waves will push us back toward shore," Paul theorized. I did not like to dash his hopes, but I was noticing that where the river waves met the lake, the two elements joined forces. The wind, too, was steadily offshore. No, we were being carried right out toward dark, mysterious Mokoia Island.

The wind was getting stronger. Our little boat was flip-flopping around, turning broadside to the waves—deep lake waves, not river current any longer. Every once in a while they would slap against the flat bottom with a shock that quivered through the boat, so that it felt as if at any moment it might break into pieces. We were both too scared to talk much. How long would the old rowboat, only meant for fishing or crossing the river, hold up in rough lake water?

"Whose boat is this, Eve?" Paul asked.

I had been wondering the same thing. Would someone miss the boat and come looking for us? "It's not Old Kate's boat," I replied. "Wrong side of the river." Then I added gloomily, "I told Mother we were going down to the lake, but I didn't say where."

Paul made no reply, and we continued on our way in silence.

After a while he spoke again. "You know what I wish, Eve? I wish we were going for Dalzie now."

Our afternoon job was to find Dalzie, our Jersey cow, who grazed free on the roadside. She wore a bell, but she was so cunning that she would stand still or even kneel in the bushes when it was time for us to fetch her, keeping so quiet that the bell would not tinkle. It was a game she played with us, and we had tired of it. I knew what Paul meant. If only we could be doing our chores instead of sitting in a boat without oars in this cold wind on the rough lake, drifting toward Mokoia Island.

"I suppose Dalzie will come home by herself sooner or later," I said guiltily. "I guess Dad will have to milk her now."

"And Mother will have to feed the chickens and gather

the eggs," said Paul, "and there'll be no wood brought in." These were his late-afternoon tasks. It was frightening to think that perhaps we would not be home tomorrow morning to light up the old black stove and to serve Mother and Dad their cups of early-morning tea in bed.

"I'm hungry," Paul added.

Somehow I felt almost as bad about his hunger as about having let us get into this danger.

"I bet if we're not home by six, Dad will come looking for us," I said cheerfully.

"And what will he find?" Paul asked. Even though he was nine, and two years younger than I, he was always the practical one. "Probably not even a broken bit of rope to give him a clue."

It was true. The boat had been tied well back in the willows. The break must have come fairly close to that point, for we had trailed a long rope behind us as we floated in the river current, and Paul and I had coiled it neatly in the bottom, as good sailors should.

"Oh, well! Maybe we'll get to Mokoia Island," I said, trying to sound optimistic.

The sun was westering, making the island a hazy purple, and far off beyond the lake, Tarawera Mountain was turning a soft rose color. The tops of the waves caught the light like diamonds. I tried not to think that it would be getting dark soon.

We were both wet from spray, and we had to keep bailing out water from the bottom, using a rusty old gooseberry preserve can that had been left in the boat, I suppose, for that purpose. The mill whistle sounded. People were going home, and dinners were being cooked.

Then we heard a motorboat.

"They're out looking for us!" Paul cried. We stood up in the boat and shouted and waved till we were hoarse. It was no use.

"Oh, why do they keep going back and forth close to shore?" I cried.

"Can't they see us?" Paul exclaimed in a voice that was keeping back tears with temper. Actually, we could barely see the motorboat, which was larger and higher than our small craft.

"Can't they figure that with no oars we'll be drifting farther and farther out?" I moaned, tears of frustration in my eyes.

But now our attention was drawn to the island. We were getting close. Its dark blur of forest had resolved itself into individual trees and rocks. Our drift, however, was carrying us to the left of its shore, toward a channel that passed into the next lake. Would we miss Mokoia and drift on and on?

Then, not very far off, we saw a place between us and the island where an old dead tree was stranded, partly out of the water.

"I'm going to swim to it," I said. I was a slightly better swimmer then Paul. I tied the end of the boat rope around my waist and dog-paddled the distance, drawing the boat after me. Paul, meanwhile, slipped over the stern, and holding on with his arms, used his legs as propellers.

It took quite a while, but we made the sunken tree and trod water. Our feet tipped the bottom.

"Hurrah! We made it," Paul crowed, joining me. We tied the boat to a stout branch of the stranded tree and started what was for us a long, hard swim—paddling, tiptoeing, and floating, till at last we climbed ashore on Mokoia's rugged beach.

‖≡‖

For a few minutes we just lay still. Then Paul scrambled up. "We're here! We made it."

"Shouldn't we plant a flag?" I quipped with an effort at gaiety.

"Come on, let's explore," said Paul. He was trying hard to sound brave and to keep our spirits up, but I knew by a glance at his clenched jaw that, like me, he was really dreadfully scared. This was the unknown land, the tabu island. What danger might lurk for us in these darkening trees?

CHAPTER TWO

Mysterious Mokoia

We looked up the slope. It was a tangle of undergrowth and forest as far as we could see. Back across the lake, in the village of Tahitahi where we lived, we could see some lights.

"Well, let's start!" Paul exclaimed. We were blue with cold. Along the shore we could go nowhere, for except where we had landed, rocky cliffs came straight down to the water. They were topped by a dense growth of scrub. But we forgot that by leaving the spot where we had landed, we were probably making our rescue more difficult.

"If we just keep climbing, we should get to the top," Paul reasoned.

"And maybe we could rub sticks together to make a signal fire," I added. I had some rather vague ideas as to how it was done.

It was tough going.

"Real adventures aren't as comfortable as make-believe ones," said Paul through still-chattering teeth.

We clawed our way through the tangle of growth, tearing pieces of clothing and even skin on the thorns of blackberry vines. In places the ferns and bushes seemed almost impenetrable.

"Listen!" I said. "What's that?"

"More pork! More pork!" sounded a weird call.

"It's just a morepork, Eve." Paul giggled with pent-up relief.

I, too, was relieved that it was just a New Zealand owl. We had been climbing quite a time now, and we knew we were high above the lake. We were tired and getting weak from hunger.

"Let's stop for a rest," said Paul. We huddled together in the increasing dusk. "It'll be moonlight soon, won't it?" Paul asked hopefully.

"I think so," I said. The stillness was frightening.

"That's funny!" Paul was suddenly alert. "I seem to smell something—something to eat!"

We sniffed the air. Yes! There was something new and curiously delicious on the breeze. We sprang up and began climbing furiously again. After a little while we came to what looked as if it might be a path.

"A path," I whispered. "And I smell smoke."

"Some Maoris out hunting, most likely," said Paul, but I noticed that he, too, kept his voice to a whisper.

"Maybe someone lives here," I replied in the same low tone. We crept along, keeping close together. In an odd way we seemed to be moving into one of the fairy tales we had read.

But now there was definitely the smell of wood smoke and of food. We came to a sharp turn in the path.

Before us, towering straight into the air, rose a great dark rock. Near its top, lashed to a stunted tree that grew gauntly from a crevice in the rock, loomed a carved wooden

Maori figure. It was moss-grown and ancient-looking, and very frightening in the dim light. Its gleaming eyes, made of shell, stared down at us, and its long tongue protruded from a gaping mouth. A club was clutched in its carved, three-fingered hand. The face was cracked with age and seemed to menace us.

We had seen such figures before, of course; there were carvings not unlike it in the public gardens at the nearby town of Rotorua. But in this setting and in the dim light, the effect was terrifying.

At the base of the rock, in a bag of flax like those the Maoris braid for carrying things, were sweet potatoes— *kumara*—the main food of the Maori people. This was what we had smelled for so long—steaming hot and fragrant.

But we were too frightened to feel hungry, even at the sight of this delicious food. We stood as if we, too, were carved wooden images.

Suddenly the figure seemed to come alive. Below it a face materialized, with a shock of untidy white hair and some strong tattoo marks. Then out of the gloom a stooped and huddled old man came toward us. We saw now that he was a Maori. His face was all wrinkled; he was wearing a straggly waist mat made of New Zealand flax, and around his shoulders was a worn and tattered blanket. His gnarled feet were bare, and through a twist of flax cord tied around his head was thrust a wooden pipe.

"Tena koe!" I said in a voice that trembled slightly, using the Maori words of greeting. Then in the best Maori I could manage, I told him we had drifted to Mokoia and were lost.

"Aue!" he sympathized. The word sounded like the wail of our puppy when he wanted us to know he was sorry

‖≡‖

because we had hurt ourselves, and it gave us the same sense of comfort. "Come," he continued, and he led the way around the great rock along the path. His wrinkles were nice, friendly ones that fitted well into his tattoo marks, and now we were not at all afraid of him. He smiled and beckoned to us reassuringly. We followed.

He took us to a shelter, half cave and half thatched hut formed in the side of the rock on the far side from the path.

"Who are you, Grandfather?" I asked politely, in the Maori way. I was so glad Dad had taught me to speak a little of the Maori language.

"I am the *tohunga*, Tawhia," he replied, by which he meant he was a priest of the old Maori religion and his name was Tawhia.

"I live here alone," he continued, "for all the rest of my people are now Christians. After me no one will secure the *kumara* crop for the Maori of the lake district. If I did not tend the *kumara* god, the crops of the Maori around here would wither and die. Ah, well! Perhaps I am just a foolish old man.

"But come. We will climb the hill to the place of fire, and the people of Tahitahi will see the signal we shall make and will come for you."

"My father will know, and he will come," said Paul.

"Your father, is he the storekeeper who used to be the doctor-missionary, Martini Kingi?" asked Tawhia. We nodded. Our father was Martin King.

"Yes, you speak the Maori tongue. Yes, I think your father will know, and he will come."

By now a curious hope was making me watch the old man's movements breathlessly. Would he get a fireboard with a groove in it for making fire? And when we got to the place of fire, would he rub a dry stick along the groove after he had sprinkled it with little pieces of dry wood—back and forth, back and forth—till the wood became hot and the splinters caught fire in the old Maori way? That was how Dad had told me it was done, and I wanted to see it happen.

But through the trees, close by, we saw the glow from his own fire, on a little hearth with a shelter over it. So of course all he did was go over to it and pick out a partly burned piece of wood as a torch.

Tawhia blew on it till it was flaming gently and gave it to Paul to hold. He then stooped and went into the hut through the low entrance. Soon he came out again with two warm flax capes of the kind the Maoris braid so skillfully. He put them around our shoulders. Then he passed to each of us a larged cooked *kumara*, still warm and delicious.

"Come," he said, taking the torch back from Paul and expertly blowing it to vigorous light again. The three of us started climbing upward on a continuation of the path by which we had come.

As we climbed, Tawhia continued to blow gently from time to time on the burning piece of wood. Its flickering glow sent lights and shadows dancing among the trees, which had hanging vines, ferns, and grasslike plants growing from the crotches of their branches. Wherever the trees thinned out, there rose tall, umbrella-like tree ferns. The bush, as New Zealanders call the forest, looked more eerie than ever by torchlight. But we no longer felt afraid.

Soon we came out on the shoulder of the hill that formed the center of the island. We were above the treetops at last. We could see the lake. The moon was making a path across it, touching all the little waves with silver.

Tawhia led us to a place on a great outcropping of rock,

where we could tell many fires had been burned. Indeed, there were some piles of cut wood ready to be lit.

"Gather small pieces of wood to begin the fire," the old Maori commanded. Soon there was an enormous wood stack, as high as Paul's head, carefully constructed by Tawhia.

I was feeling tense again. Here was our hope of rescue. Would it carry its message over the lake? We watched intently as Tawhia set the torch to it. In almost no time a great fire sent crimson flames leaping high into the sky.

"How long before they come?" asked Paul in a drowsy voice.

"Not long," I assured him. "They'll see it from the motor-boat." Then I added, "I think Dad and Mother will understand, don't you? They must be terribly worried. But I don't think they'll be really angry with us." My voice was not as sure as I wanted it to be.

"I'm not worried about that," said Paul. "I just want to get home. I'm so tired."

We huddled together on the rock beside the fire, which Tawhia continued to feed with pieces of wood from his pile. My anxiety began to slip away in the friendly warmth. This was exciting, really, for I knew this way of sending messages was thousands of years old, and this message was all about us. Soon we were asleep.

We were awakened by the noise of a puttering motor-boat. I tried to stay awake, but I must have dropped off again, for the next thing I heard was Dad's voice, talking in Maori to old Tawhia. Then Dad just gathered me up in his arms, big girl though I was. I waved to Tawhia, who was standing by the fire. Paul's head was jogging ahead of us on Uncle David's shoulder.

Presently Paul straightened up and said, "The boat! We

‖≡‖

must get the rowboat. And put me down! We can walk, can't we?"

"Yes," I said, "we'll show you where." Practical Paul! I think I would have forgotten all about the rowboat. I scrambled out of Dad's comforting arms somewhat self-consciously.

We were now fully awake and alert. To our surprise the path on which Paul and I had stumbled in our upward climb ran all the way down to the shore, where there was a plank landing place at which the motor launch was tied. We piloted our rescue party to where our rowboat nestled against the half-submerged tree. Once it was secured behind the launch, the questioning began.

"How did you get the boat?" asked Dad. We told him and Uncle David our story.

"It was a foolish thing to do," said Uncle David, "getting into a boat on a flooded river."

"You frightened us out of a year of our lives," Dad admitted.

"I'm glad the boat didn't come untied this time," I said, proud at least of our seamanship.

"I think," Dad continued, ignoring my remark, "we shall have to restrict you to our own property for a month to teach you to be more responsible."

"Oh, Dad!" groaned Paul. I could see alarm in his eyes as they caught mine. The long school vacation had just begun, and to be confined to our own backyard was unthinkable!

"Perhaps," said Uncle David softly, "this experience has made them think. Maybe it has been the punishment, no?" Dear Uncle David! In all our scrapes he was "lawyer for the defense."

We waited breathlessly. Dad did not reply at once. Then

he said, "Let's hope this is your last adventure for a long time." He said no more about punishment. I had a strange feeling of being almost regretful. "At least I'll never let Paul get into danger like this again," I said to myself. Dad drew me to him with the arm that was free of the tiller, and I relaxed against him.

We landed at the beach, which was lined with villagers, relatives, and friends. Mother was standing there.

Then there was only Mother, holding us to her and saying softly, "Thank God." I had never felt before how much I loved her. She was warm and close as when we were small —not busy and efficient and rather hard to understand, as she had seemed lately.

As we stepped off the launch onto the crude landing planks that served as a wharf, Dad called to the Maori man Pita Tawa, who was standing nearby, leaning on his crutches.

"Thank you, Pita. We'll always be grateful."

"Why, what did Pita do?" asked Paul quickly.

"He saw you go off toward the river," Dad replied, "and remembered—so we went out there and found the rowboat gone. It's Pita's boat that he hires out to fishermen."

"Thank you, Pita," my brother and I called in chorus. We did not guess there would be other times when that strange figure would loom over us in ways both good and evil. I thought I caught an amused and wicked gleam in his eyes as they met mine. But I was too tired, at the close of our first brush with real danger, to think about it.

CHAPTER THREE

Paul Disappears

It was December, summer in the Southern Hemisphere, and our school vacation stretched invitingly before us. Of course, we helped in the store, which our parents owned and which served as a community center as well.

Our parents had come to Tahitahi as medical missionaries to the Maoris. They were the first white people in the valley and ran a small school and clinic as part of the mission. The Maoris used to share their good catches of fish and their crops with Mother and Dad; but later, with two children to raise, our parents found this kind of support unpredictable. Dad then built the store with a two-story house attached to it and a big warehouse essential for stocking farm supplies.

Paul and I weighed and measured articles, packed up goods for customers, and refilled the shelves when the stock ran low. Mother and Dad had me do the accounts of the store, but of course one of them always checked my figures.

There was time, though, to ramble through the countryside. We went bird-nesting. We knew the eggs of the local birds: the white eggs of the kingfisher in the little cave so carefully excavated in the riverbank; the blue-green eggs of the thrush in convenient low bushes easy to peek into; the camouflaged eggs of the lark in its carefully hidden nest in old, dried tussock grass, so difficult to find; the carefree, deep, soft sparrow's nest, wonderfully warm with its downy feather lining for the mottled gray-brown eggs; and high in the acacia trees, which we called wattles, the exquisite small nest of the fantail, lined with horsehair and disguised outside with lichen and moss, holding within it the daintiest little eggs of all.

We fed and cared for fledglings that had fallen too soon from the nest. Our yard had an assortment of cages in it, homemade from old packing cases, and we learned what foods to give our little refugees. Seeing them hop and fly away, launched by our efforts into maturity, was a joy— and somewhat of an achievement, too, since our yard was home also to dogs and cats.

The happy, contented routine of living, however, was broken for me during the last weeks of that summer. I was eleven and lived part of the time in a mist of fear. It began with the earthquakes. The first one came as Paul and I were helping Dad unload cases of groceries from a flatcar down at the railway station. We were shifting the cases onto a truck.

"Hey! Stop pushing there!" called Dad. He thought someone was pushing the truck. Then he realized it was something much bigger than a push. The ground around us, and the bottom of the truck beneath us, seemed to be rocking and waving in great shudders. I reached for Dad and clung to him.

"It's nothing!" Dad said. "Just an earthquake. But a really big one this time."

I suppose I must have been in small earthquakes before,

but I had never noticed them. Now, suddenly, the earth seemed mysteriously alive and no longer dependable.

"You goose!" Paul laughed at me. "See, I'm not afraid! Earthquakes are just natural, aren't they, Dad?"

The earthquake did not feel "just natural" to me. For a week there were more—all terrifying to me. Lying in bed at night, I would find it difficult to go to sleep, and I would wonder if the quakes meant that we were going to be destroyed the way the people were in the Bible story about the burning cities of the plain in the time of Lot. But at last they subsided.

That week, too, the wind, which in Tahitahi almost always blew from the hills, fresh with the tang of the bush, came instead, hot and heavy, from Rotorua town. It smelled like rotten eggs. That was sulphur, Dad said.

As long as I could remember, I had been afraid of Rotorua and of the thermal wonders that people from all over the world came there to see: the geysers of scalding water rising hundreds of feet into the air like giant feathers of water and steam; the plop-plopping pools of boiling mud; the hissing steam holes and cracks; the banks of yellow sulphur that looked like jewels in the sun; the streams that ran with hot and cold currents in the same bed. Whenever we had visited Whaka (Whakarewarewa), the public reserve and Maori village on one side of the town of Rotorua where these wonders were most concentrated, I would cling closely to Dad's or Mother's hand as we stepped along well-marked trails. I was always glad to get home to Tahitahi, where things were "natural."

"I wish we didn't have to go to church in Rotorua tomorrow," I said to Paul one Saturday.

"Perhaps we could persuade them to let us spend this

Sunday with Uncle David," Paul suggested. Uncle David did not go to church. We knew in a vague way that he belonged to a different religion. He was not our true uncle, but had played that role most of our childhood. He was especially good to our cousin Alan, whose own father had separated from Aunt Millie. We knew that Uncle David wanted Aunt Millie to get a divorce and marry him, which would have made him our real uncle, but Aunt Millie would not make up her mind. Uncle David, a widower, lived alone in a little cottage by the river, where he loved to fish in the evenings and on weekends. Often he took us fishing with him, fixing our flies and casts with endless patience when we needed help. It would be great fun to spend a whole Sunday with him.

But our parents thought otherwise.

"We'll take a basket of good things to old Rivers," Mother said, "and we'll picnic in the sanatorium grounds after church." These were the beautiful gardens of Rotorua, which surrounded a great bath building where visitors could bathe in different kinds of bubbling hot mineral water, and even in the warm mud. Paul and I always laughed at the thought of that. But these baths were supposed to restore youth, health, and beauty, so people crowded to them. Old Rivers was a small gnome of a man, bent and crippled with rheumatism. He lived all by himself beside his favorite hot pool, in a tiny hut built in the scrub at the edge of the public gardens.

"Can we have tea and French pastries in the kiosk, Mother? And can we feed bits of bread to the sparrows?" I asked.

"Can we feed the goldfish?" Paul asked. These were large old carp living in the pools among the water lilies.

‖≡‖

"Of course," said Mother, answering us both, "and we'll invite Aunt Millie and Alan to come with us."

It did sound like fun, and I tried to put away my fears.

That Sunday afternoon, while the grownups were resting after lunch in the shade of the trees, not far from the place where old Rivers had his hut, Alan and Paul and I played hide-and-seek.

"Keep on the paths and lawns. Don't go into the scrub," Dad warned us. "There are hot pools through it."

"As if I needed this warning," I thought.

After we had been playing quite a time, Alan called to me, "Where's Paul? I can't find him anywhere!" It was his turn to seek. He had found me and counted me out long since.

"He went down that path," I told him, pointing to the trail that led through the scrub to old Rivers' hut. So Alan and I started to search together.

"Aren't those his shoe marks?" I asked.

"I think so," said Alan as we turned off onto a branching path.

"I'm scared," I said. "Let's go back and get Dad." I could hear hissing and bubbling steam vents close by, and the smell of sulphur that I hated so much was strong.

"Paul! Paul!" Alan shouted. Then we both shouted together. There was no reply.

My heart was thumping now. What if Paul had fallen into a boiling pool! We ran back to our parents and Aunt Millie.

"Paul is lost!" Alan shouted in a frightened voice as we came near enough to be heard. We quickly told about the shoe marks on the trail through the scrub. In a moment the search was on.

"You two stay right here," Dad commanded us. "From now on grownups will do the looking."

We sat down on the grass and waited, sick with fear. Alan's pleasant face looked pale, and the freckles showed more than usual. "He was stupid to go along a path into the scrub!" he said. "Uncle Martin told us not to."

"Shh! Listen!" I begged him.

Dad's voice was carrying all over the area, but we heard no reply. Waiting there was dreadful—much worse than searching.

Then suddenly we heard Mother's voice, in a loud, glad cry. "I've found him, Martin. He's here in Rivers' hut, and he's all right!"

We all ran down the path to the little thatched hut. Paul was stretched out on the earth floor with closed eyes, and Mother was kneeling beside him, feeling his head. The old man hobbled to a seat.

"He was running down the path," he told us in a quavery, high-pitched voice. "Not this one—the one just through the scrub there"—he pointed—"but the earthquake has opened up a new vent, right across it. He didn't see till he nearly fell in. Then when he tried to stop himself, he twisted his ankle and fell. He hit his head on a rock."

"How ever did he get *here*?" asked Mother.

"I heard him cry out as he fell, so I went to him and carried him back," said Rivers simply.

"You *carried* him?" Dad exclaimed. It seemed unbelievable. The frail, bent old man moved as slowly as a turtle.

"I don't know how I did it, either," he admitted. "When I got him here, I was too spent to call out, even though I heard you calling."

We could believe that.

"I was afraid to leave him there," said Rivers. "He might've slipped into a hole as he came to. The whole earth is thin and crumbling there. It's a bad place. Other holes keep opening up. So I tried. And I was stronger than I thought. The ground is solid here."

"I saw the place," said Dad. "I thought we would never see our boy again."

Paul was stirring now and trying to sit up.

"Where am I?" he asked. "Ouch!" he added as he went to move his foot.

"You'll be fine when we get that ankle braced up," said Dad. "I'll carry you on my back for a bit." As we left, we all smothered the old man in thanks and good wishes, but to me the power beneath our thin earth crust now seemed to lurk as a personal enemy.

CHAPTER FOUR

The Sacrifice

Paul was none the worse for his adventure, and in just a few days he was able to get around on his ankle again. Unlike me, he did not even seem to think back to the moment when he stopped himself on the crumbling edge of that steaming hole. In the daytime, I tried to throw off my fears, but at night I would imagine the area where Paul had fallen, all the more clearly because I had not actually seen the place. I would break out in a sweat that soaked my bed.

"My ankle's strong again, Eve. Can't we visit our cave today?" Paul asked at breakfast one morning. This was something we had wanted to do once more before school began again the next week.

"I'm sure there's more to it than what we saw when we took Aunt Millie," Paul continued. "There might even be another cave along the cliff face." We loved to climb the steep slopes of Tahitahi Mountain.

"If we do find another opening, we won't go in out of sight of the entrance," I said firmly. I was not in the mood just then for an adventure.

"I promise," he replied. "We won't even take candle ends. I only want to look."

‖≡‖

Our parents gave permission, and we took some lunch along so that we would not have to hurry home. Instead of cutting across country, we took the road toward Rotorua for about a half-mile and then the side road up the mountain slope to the cemetery. Many of the graves were overgrown with ti tree and bracken, but some were bright with flowers. We rested beneath a marble angel.

"Look how the lake has streaks of color in it today," I said, "and there's smoke from the top of Mokoia."

But Paul's eyes were on the mountain slope. "Look at that tall gravestone highest up of all," he said. "I'm going to see whose it is."

I accompanied him. Soon, beneath the tall column of gray granite, we stood reading the inscription.

"In memory of all those who lost their lives in the eruption of Mount Tarawera," it said, and there was a long list of names and the story of how a whole village had been buried in hot rocks and ash and how almost all the people of the town had perished.

Paul and I looked over to where Tarawera Mountain rose pearly gray in the distance beyond the lake.

"Will our Tahitahi Mountain ever erupt?" I asked with a tremor in my voice.

"Oh, come on to the cave," said Paul.

But there really did seem to be very little to our cave. Search as we would, we could find no further passages, nor any other cave in the cliff face. We ate our sandwiches and drank the fruit juice we had carried with us in a bottle and were ready to start home.

"Look," said Paul, pointing above our heads to a shelf-like projection. "I think those are some bones on a kind of shelf." I gave him a hoist up so that he could explore.

"Gosh! I think they're human bones!" he said, looking a

‖≡‖‖

little sick. "And there's a bashed-in skull right back there against the rock." By this time we had noticed that there were many high, shelflike projections. Perhaps there were bones on all of them; indeed, we thought we could see some more. Our cave began to feel like part of the cemetery below it.

"Let's go!" said Paul.

We hurried down the slope, past the graves, hot with sun, and out to the main road for home. As we reached the highway, we saw Pita Tawa sitting on the bank, smoking his pipe. He had laid his crutches down beside him.

"Pita," I exclaimed, "what are you doing here?"

"I wait, catch a lift to Rotorua maybe." Pita loved to catch rides; it was his main way of getting around.

"Where you been?" he asked.

We told him about the cave. "Are those Maori bones up there?" Paul asked.

"Yes, Maori bones," said Pita, "bones of my people, not in the monument like white people. They die in Tarawera eruption."

"Were they your own people, Pita, not just Maori people?" asked my brother sharply.

"My people. I just little boy. That way I lose my leg," Pita replied. "That cave up there, home place Volcano God."

Pita's sharp dark eyes were no longer sly. They were terrifying, with little fires in them, and he was looking hard at me, as if he could see right through me.

"One day soon, this mountain blow top off, all over Tahitahi. All die."

Cold shivers ran up my spine. "When, Pita?" I asked, though my mouth was so dry that I found it hard to move my tongue and lips.

"Any day now. Any day big fires come out of Tahitahi."

"Can't anything be done?" I asked.

"*You* can do a thing," said Pita, looking at me harder than ever. "Maybe you save Tahitahi."

"How, Pita?"

"You take gift, maybe money, maybe jewel, some very good thing. You bury in earth of cave for Volcano God."

"Why don't you make a gift, Pita, and save Tahitahi?" said my brother, fixing Pita with an unbelieving look.

"Pita no have good gift," the Maori replied. "Maybe Volcano God take gift from Eve; maybe no fires come from Tahitahi."

"Come on home, Eve," said Paul, pulling at my arm.

"Good-bye, Pita," I said. "We hope you get a ride to Rotorua."

"The old humbug!" said my brother angrily as soon as

we were out of earshot. "He's not old enough to have been in the Tarawera eruption. He just wants you to bury something so he can steal it."

"Oh, no! Don't say that!" I exclaimed in distress, for I really liked Pita, and I had believed him.

"How could Pita possibly get up to the cave with those crutches?" I asked. Pita's words had fitted only too well into my nighttime fears. Clammy shudders were still playing along my back, and I could not get those burning eyes of his out of my mind. Tahitahi might soon be destroyed, like Tarawera, I kept thinking; and Dad, Mother, Paul, and I and all our friends would be buried in the hot lava.

When we reached home, we found Dad and asked him about the Tarawera eruption, but for some reason we kept to ourselves what Pita had said about burying a treasure in the cave.

"Pita may very well have lost his leg as a child in the eruption," Dad told us. "I've heard that story before. I know Pita is older than he looks. It might account for the way he seems to belong everywhere but nowhere among the Maoris, with no really close kinsmen. He stays in one Maori village for a time and then moves on to another."

"Dad, will Tahitahi ever blow up like Tarawera?" I asked.

"I suppose it could happen, but it isn't likely," he replied. "I wouldn't worry about it."

But I did worry. That night I could not fall asleep. In the darkness everything seemed to get out of proportion. I felt I had to do something, as Pita had said, and suddenly I knew what it was.

Grandma had sent me a brooch for my eleventh birthday. In its beautiful dark-blue, plush-lined case it lay in the top drawer of the bureau chest in the corner of my bedroom. I got it out and sat looking at it in the moonlight. It was mainly gold, in the shape of a lily of the valley leaf and flower stalk. The leaf had a fine layer of green enamel on it, and each of the three little flower buds was a real pearl. I loved it. But here was the treasure I had to bury, and I had to do it at once, this very night, or I would not be able to part with it. Tomorrow might be too late; the volcano could erupt any time. In the darkness it seemed urgent that I act at once.

I put on the warmest clothes I could lay hands on in what moonlight found its way into the room. I did not need any lantern.

Then I set out. It was very cold, and running seemed a good idea. It would get me back more quickly to my warm bed. Soon I was out of breath, but it did not seem to take me very long to reach the point where we had talked with Pita. I turned up the side road to the cemetery.

This was the worst part of the trip. The graves at night were peaceful-looking, but so cold and lonely that they gave me shivers, and I found I was tiptoeing and holding my breath. The moonlight was fading in the dim half-light of dawn, and the horizon line was getting brighter. Each bush in the graveyard seemed to hold a weird shape. But there was no sound to frighten me, not even a morepork.

It was difficult climbing in the dim light up above the cemetery to the cave, but I knew the way from our morning trip and made it without getting too scratched up by the bracken. The cave seemed peaceful and serene.

"It'd be nicer to have your bones lie here," I thought, "than down there under a stone in the cemetery."

Not letting myself stop to think, I made a small hole in

the dusty earth floor with a stick. Then I quickly laid in it my precious plush-lined box, with its treasure within, and covered it over with the fine dust. I found a stone and put it on the top, marking the place.

I hurried down the mountainside, through the cemetery, and out to the main road. It seemed colder than ever. Even though this was summertime, my teeth were chattering. With the approaching day, what I had done began to look silly to me, and I was filled with doubts. I was of half a mind to climb back up to the cave and recover my treasure, but I needed to get back home and into bed, for by this time I was shivering all over.

"I'm so glad no one need ever know I did this," I said to myself as I crept back safely into my bedroom. It took a long time to get warm, even in bed, but at last I fell deeply asleep. Paul had to shake me awake for breakfast.

Only a few days after that I became ill, with almost the only illness I can ever remember having.

The doctor said I had diphtheria. Dad and Mother wore anxious faces and spent many days carefully nursing me. Paul could not come to see me, but I was much too sick to want play or companionship anyway. In my head a great buzzing went on and on, like a swarm of mosquitoes or the grinding sound of many wheels.

Gradually I got well and spent pleasant days convalescing. I could draw and paint and at last was allowed to read.

On my mind much of the time was my precious brooch, lying up there in the earth of the cave. I longed to be well again so that I could climb to the cave and dig it up. I no longer felt afraid that the mountain would become a volcano. The fears seemed to have left me, along with my fever.

At last I was completely recovered.

"Mother," I said, when I thought I might possibly be allowed out alone, "I'd like to go for an early-morning walk, all by myself. I want to watch the sunrise tomorrow."

"Why, of course you may, dear, only put on a warm jacket and don't go too far—and sit down and rest every now and then. I'm so glad my funny little girl can watch a sunrise again!" Mother replied. "We'll keep some breakfast hot for you. Don't overdo it, though. I don't want you to have to miss much more school, or it may be hard to catch up with the class." It was true I had already missed the opening weeks of school.

"I won't go far," I promised her. "But I may not be back to have breakfast with you all."

Next morning I could not get away fast enough. I was afraid Paul, or even Alan, would be sent to look after me. I kept looking back to make sure I was not being followed.

I had to rest every once in a while, for I was not really as strong yet as I thought I was. But in due course I came to the cemetery and climbed up to our cave in the crisp sunlight of early morning.

My heart hammered against my ribs as my fingers pried into the soil beneath the stone. I dug and dug. I found nothing there. I tried other places around the stone. Soon I had torn up all the earth on the floor of the cave. I dug through it all, over and over, unable to believe that my treasure was really gone. But at last I knew there could be no mistake. My plush-lined box and its contents had disappeared. I knew it had been taken, and not by the Volcano God. In the clear light of day and health I knew full well that Pita's Volcano God did not exist. Who had taken it? Surely not Pita! He could never have climbed up to the cave—of that I felt certain. Had he sent some other children here to find it? I would probably never know. And Pita! How would I be able to look at him again? Though I could not figure how, I could not down the feeling that he was involved in this disappearance. This hurt me almost as much as the loss of my treasure.

I sat down at the cave entrance, and hot tears blinded me. I could still feel and see my lovely brooch.

Slowly I made my way down to the cemetery. I sat for a time beneath the great monument for the dead of the Tarawera eruption.

The morning light was making the lake a lovely sheet of glass. Mokoia Island looked so near that I felt I could reach out my hand and touch it. Peace started to steal over me. I no longer seemed to be afraid, and I thought I would never again be afraid in my whole life.

"Fear makes you stupid," I said to myself. My brooch was perhaps a small price for this new wisdom.

I made my way home, resting often in the pleasant sunshine. My breakfast had been kept warm for me. I was glad I had kept this episode to myself, for I felt, above all, very foolish.

"Dad," I said at lunchtime, "can we go to Rotorua this Sunday and see the geysers again?"

"Why, Eve! I thought you were afraid of them!"

"Not any more, Dad," I replied confidently.

||三||三||三||三||三||三||三||三||三||三||三||三||三||三||三||三||三||三||三||三||三||三||

Green Paint

"I detest old Froggie!" I exclaimed to Paul one day when I got home from school. "He's mean! He caned Billy Hodge again today just because he didn't get enough spelling words right. It makes me so mad. I don't think Billy and some of the others can do any better, no matter how hard they try." In my mind I could still hear the whining swish of the strap as it cut through the air, and the dull thud as it landed on the soft palm. "Froggie hauls the kids out and lays on, and his face gets redder and redder," I added. "Froggie" was our disrespectful name for Mr. Froggin, the only teacher I ever disliked. He was headmaster of our three-teacher school and taught the upper classes.

"He hasn't ever strapped you, Eve, has he?" Paul asked.

"Not yet," I replied, wondering whether I really wanted him to, just to prove that our dislike was mutual. "I wonder," I thought, "if I could bear it."

"He'd better not," Paul growled. Then he added mischievously, "Teacher's pet!"

"Don't say that!" I exclaimed fiercely. "Someday I'll do something dreadful to him. I do like school though, don't you, Paul?"

"Oh yes, and we have fun at recess, don't we?"

‖≣‖

Paul was the best sprinter in his age group and was good at cricket. He was a handsome boy, with bright golden hair and deep-set hazel eyes under strong brown lashes. His face seemed rather pale, but that was probably because of the startling, dark brightness of his eyes. Watching him as he swung his bat at cricket, pretty Mavis Hodge with her madcap curls, or the half-caste Ruti, who was a beauty of the school, would exclaim loudly enough for him to hear, "That Paul King is just too handsome!" and they would giggle together. I would know, even though he pretended to take no notice, that Paul had heard, for he would try extra hard to distinguish himself.

Two of my girl friends were Maoris, the sisters Rangi and Pari. Rangi was plump, good-natured, and gay, with a rather dark complexion, nearly black flashing eyes, and long, heavy ropes of braided black hair. Pari was slender, and her skin was more fair. She had soft brown eyes and curly brown hair. She was more serious than Rangi and often looked discontented. We all respected her quick, sharp temper.

"Dare you to go as high as we can!" Pari or Rangi would call, and they would start together, standing up on the seat of our extremely tall school swing, facing each other and working the swing up to speed and height. I would try, and so would the others, standing or sitting, singly or in pairs. But Pari and Rangi always went the highest, till the ropes slackened in a dizzying way in midair before the return pendulum swing. The girls always kept control. Once I tried with Pari as my partner, but I was terrified and dizzy before she reached her full swing level, and I had to beg her to let me off.

They tried to teach me to do the Maori *poi* dances. A *poi* is a ball on the end of a cord, made of braided flax leaf

‖≣‖

fibers. The dancer holds one of these balls by the cord in each hand and twirls them both in spinning, whirling patterns as she sings and dances. I never did learn, but I marveled at their grace and skill and their patience in trying to teach me. "My legs and arms won't behave properly together," I said. The strings in my hands, holding the *poi* balls, were short on magic. The balls would stop spinning and hang limp, or would fly up and hit me in the eye, or I would forget to accompany them with the dance movements. Eventually, I gave up trying.

Sometimes I would play rugby with the boys. One way or another I would usually arrive home with my clothes torn and a collection of cuts, scratches, and bruises all over.

"You should have been a boy!" Mother would say with a sigh.

One day I rushed home from school panting and red-faced, with terror in my eyes.

"Oh, Paul!" I cried—his class got out earlier than mine— "I'm in real trouble. Mr. Froggin is going to tell Dad about it on his way home!"

"Whatever did you do to Froggie?" Paul asked, amazed that his older sister could be delinquent.

"Well, it's hard to explain. Today he strapped Billy Hodge again—for making arithmetic mistakes this time. He yanked him out and strapped him. I was paint monitor, and the last period of the afternoon was coming up. I was mixing green paint powder with water so each desk could get a glassful.

"So I mixed up an extra pint of paint, thick and gooey and green. Every morning, when Froggie comes in, he does a flip with his hat and makes it land on top of that tall hall closet; he's too short to reach up there properly, and usually it lands upside-down. Then when he leaves in the after-

noon, he does a little hop and catches it by the rim, pulling it right down on his head."

"Oh, no!" Paul interrupted me, slapping his knees with anticipatory delight, his eyes gleaming with a mixture of joy and horror. "You didn't really fill his hat with paint!"

"Oh, yes I did! And it worked beautifully!" In spite of my fears I, too, began to laugh at the remembrance, and we held each other and rolled around with glee.

"You should have seen the green slime running all over his ugly red face and down onto his suit! It was a terrible mess!"

"Did he know who did it?" Paul asked when we had sobered down again.

"Of course. I was the only one who could have done it."

"What did he say? What did the other kids say?"

"The ones who were there were all too scared and surprised even to laugh," I replied. "Most had already gone home." Then I added, "But Billy Hodge was there. You should have seen his face! Horror and happiness all mixed up! And Fred Lambeth was there," I continued, "and he whispered to me, 'Good for you—but get out of here quickly!' So I started to dash down the front steps, but Froggie called after me, 'I'll see your father on my way home!'"

"He'll be coming by any minute, then," said Paul.

"Yes," I groaned. "I guess he's cleaning himself up now as best he can."

"Dad's out by the road mending the gate," Paul said. "Do you want me to go out and help him so I can hear and report to you?"

"Oh, no, Paul, stay with me," I pleaded. "We'll watch from the living room window."

We waited there, looking through the curtains, and presently along came that pompous, stubby figure, looking more bull-necked than ever. His suit was wet and crumpled, and even from where we were we could see green paint. He stopped when he reached Dad and began to talk to him. They were too far away for us to hear anything.

My heart was pounding so hard and fast that it hurt. I expected Dad to call or to come in to find me. But they talked on and on, first one, then the other. There were no signs of any excitement. Paul and I were both puzzled.

I knew Mr. Froggin was aware we were watching. I saw him look up from time to time at the window, and I even caught his eye twice through the open lacework curtain. The suspense was the most dreadful punishment he could have inflicted. He must have talked there nearly an hour while I cowered like a mouse under the paw of the cat.

At last he walked on, and Dad completed his work on the gate, while I waited, sick at heart, thinking my punishment was being stored up for me. Dinnertime came. We sat down as usual, and grace was said. There were still no signs of storm.

"I saw you talking with Mr. Froggin for a long time," Mother said. "What was it all about, Martin?"

"Oh, just some matters he wants me, as chairman of the school board, to put on the agenda for the next meeting, Alice. I'll tell you about them later. He'd had an accident and spilled some green paint on himself, poor fellow. I can't understand how. He'd just about ruined his suit. I hope it can be cleaned."

Paul and I sat silent and avoided each other's eyes.

"I wonder why he didn't tell Dad," Paul marveled later when we were by ourselves again.

"Maybe he wanted to hide the way he lost his dignity," I replied.

"Maybe he didn't want you to tell the chairman of the school board how he caned Billy and the other kids who can't do their work well," Paul shrewdly suggested.

It was years later before we told our parents the true story of the green paint—after we were too old to be punished.

||≡||≡||≡||≡||≡||≡||≡||≡||≡||≡||≡||≡||≡||≡||≡||≡||≡||≡||≡||≡||≡||

CHAPTER SIX

The Lambeths

Our best friends were the Lambeths. They lived on a farm about four miles up toward the hills. The children rode to school, two to a pony, or as we called it, double-banked. The ponies were corralled in a yard that was part of the school grounds.

The Lambeths were the only family we were ever allowed to stay with overnight. They had seven children and had emigrated from England, but Mr. Lambeth had died suddenly several years before we children had become close friends. People expected Mrs. Lambeth to sell the farm and return to the "old country," but instead she and the children stayed and made the farm one of the best in the district.

"I want our children to grow up in this new land," she said to Mother one day, "just as my husband and I planned together.

The eldest boy, Dick, was a grown man now and had taken over much of his father's responsibilities. The two youngest were Clive and Ann. Fred was in my class at school. He had large, warm brown eyes with curling lashes and shining brown hair. To me, he seemed too shy and gentle for a boy. I liked him, though, and I know he liked me. When we did something at school that we thought was notable, we looked at one another for approval. Fred teased me when any other boy was around, but if we were alone, we were usually both too shy to speak.

Fred had another older brother, Claude, who was a hunchback. I tried not to be sorry for Claude because I felt he was too fine to be pitied. In spite of his deformity, he had worked so hard that he was immensely strong, especially in the arms. He did his full share and more of the farm work, and at night he studied. He used to write poetry, and sometimes I persuaded him to read some of his work to me. One verse I particularly liked was:

> *"Intricate flowers of grass!*
> *My eyes are too large for them, alas.*
> *Hugely I pass."*

My special friend was Mabel, a year younger than Fred and me, and in the class just below us. She seemed to me the most wonderful person I had ever known. Her long, heavy hair fell to her waist in a honey-gold "waterfall," though ordinarily she wore it in braids or a ponytail. Everything that called for skill and grace she seemed to do superbly. She won the races and jumps at the school picnics, and at the Rotorua Show she had carried off the top prize for horsemanship as long as I had known her.

She had all the poise I longed to have but lacked, and yet she was gentle and modest, and fun to be with. She used to tease me about both Fred and Claude being in love with me.

My brother's closest friend in the family was Larry, who was his own age and in his class. Larry was a lot like Mabel and had the high color and the tendency to blush that was characteristic of the Lambeths.

The Lambeth children rode horses as naturally as they walked. Mrs. Lambeth was a fine horsewoman and had trained them all to ride well. I would get on a pony behind Mabel, Paul would climb on behind Fred or Larry, and we would race. But Paul and I just hung on. We had learned to ride on workhorses and knew little about the finer points of riding.

The Lambeths' big farm kitchen served as living room and dining room; the "sitting room" in the front of the house was hardly ever used. Next to the big coal-burning black stove of the kitchen was a very wide, open fireplace, where a huge fire burned. We quite filled the long table at dinner. The joking and teasing seemed strange to us; we were used to a more formal meal, starting with grace and consisting of rather quiet conversation, mainly between our parents.

"My biceps won't support this plate of scones," Fred ribbed Mabel. "What's in 'em, nails?"

"Try these, Eve," said Dick. "We've been saving 'em for you all week." He passed me a platter of delicious meat balls. "They're snippets of the calves' ears we've been clipping; they're especially well ground up."

Each Lambeth rose at will from the table to help serve and clear and stack dishes, so there seemed to be endless motion, like a game of musical chairs. Mountains of good food were served and eaten. For breakfast the next morning Mrs. Lambeth and Mabel cooked lamb chops, thick slices of bacon, and fried eggs in addition to the large, steaming pot-ful of porridge. There was an endless supply of good home-made bread, butter, and jam.

By eight in the morning, of course, we were all ready for this big breakfast. We had been up since the gray dawn, around five o'clock. Paul and I had ridden with Mabel and

Larry to round up and bring in the cows for milking. It was hand-milking, and we all took a share in it.

"My hands and fingers ache so," Paul confided to me as he struggled to complete stripping his one cow. I was used to milking Dalzie at home, so by ignoring the aches and trying very hard, I managed three cows that morning.

Then we separated the milk from the cream through a machine that fascinated Paul. I helped Mabel feed the young calves with some of the skimmed milk separated out in this way, while Paul and Larry fed the young pigs with more of the milk and some table scraps as well.

We all helped to clean the pails and make the cowshed immaculate. The concrete floor had to be hosed and brushed clean, and all the pails and the parts of the separator that parted the cream from the milk had to be washed well and then scalded.

While we had been helping with the milking, the two older boys had been out in the fields plowing and harrowing. They were preparing to sow a second crop on a piece of their land. We seemed to have done a day's work by eight o'clock that morning.

While we were having breakfast, Dick said, "Ma, guess who bought a horse from us yesterday."

"I don't care who, so long as he paid cash," she said, laughing.

"He did—and that's the funny part of it," replied Dick. "It was Pita Tawa. Wonder where he got the money. Anyway, I sold him the small pony—Sheila—because she's quiet, and he should have no trouble with her. She'll be easy for him to mount, too."

"I hope he's good to her," said Mabel. "I like Sheila."

"He seemed to have a way with her, I thought," said Dick.

"I'd say he's handled horses before. He'll probably make a pet of her because he seems to be a lonely sort of guy. Not like a Maori in some ways."

My cheeks were burning. Luckily no one seemed to be looking at me. Had my brooch been turned into a pony, I wondered? I felt angry. Then I felt ashamed. Shouldn't I be glad if I had helped in providing a one-legged cripple with four new strong legs? All the same, I was glad when the topic of conversation changed to the Lambeths' great discovery.

"First you must swear to eternal secrecy," said Mabel.

Paul and I swore. "I've a mosquito bite that's bleeding," I said. "We'll sign a pledge in blood!" We did it very officially.

Then they told us how just off their property about half a mile from the railroad, they had found a valley so beautiful and exciting it was hard to believe it was real. No one else except some railroad men knew about it.

"We'll tell you its name, but you must never reveal it," said Fred.

"Let's take them there next Saturday," said Larry.

"Could we get away from chores?" Mabel wondered.

"I would think so just this once," said Fred, "if we were home in time for milking."

"Let's ask Mother," Larry suggested.

Mrs. Lambeth gave her permission, and we made detailed plans.

"Walk up the railroad line from Tahitahi. It'll take the best part of an hour, I think. Then wait for us to join you when you get to the viaduct," said Fred.

"Shall we plan to be there about eleven in the morning?" I suggested. They all agreed.

"Don't forget to bring bathing suits," said Mabel.

"Bring a package of lunch, but nothing to drink," said Fred. We assumed they were planning to bring drinks.

"And now, please," I begged, "tell us the name you gave to the valley."

"Paradise Valley," they chorused.

We said it over. It sounded beautiful. Paul and I could hardly get through the week at school for dreaming and wondering about Paradise Valley.

I, however, had another matter on my mind as well. When would I see Pita Tawa riding on Sheila? How would I look at him and he at me? It was all the more disturbing because there was no one with whom I could discuss it, not even my brother.

It was only two days later that it happened. As Paul and I were on our way to school, Pita came by us on the new pony, riding at a fast amble. He sat well in the saddle, to which he had attached his crutches with special loops made of rope. He reined in and greeted us with his usual bland smile.

"How you like my new pony?" he asked.

"I like it very much, Pita," I replied.

"How fast can she go?" asked Paul.

"Very good pony," he said, fondling its neck, "I no want to go fast—she fast enough for me."

I looked enviously at Sheila. She was a soft brown, and darker around the eyes and the mane and tail. I could not help feeling deeply that she was really mine. It was at that moment that there was born in me a deep and urgent desire to have a pony of my own. Pita was looking at me with no appearance of self-consciousness, but only an eagerness to win my approval of his new possession. Surely I had no

right, no right at all, to feel suspicious. Pita nudged the pony, and she swung into a steady trot, which Pita could manage very well. As he rode off, I seemed to see him riding on a steed of green and gold, with three white pearls along the neck.

"I wish I had a pony of my own," I said to Paul with a sigh.

‖≡‖

CHAPTER SEVEN

Paradise Valley

Saturday was a perfect day with a cloudless sky, but hot for walking. Our way lay along the dusty sand and clay road to where it intersected the railroad. Then we headed up the tracks. At last we came in sight of the viaduct. As soon as the Lambeths saw us coming, they stood up and yelled, "Ya hoo!"

We shouted back and soon joined them.

"Come on," said Fred. "Let's cross the viaduct."

"Oh, no!" exclaimed Paul. "Can't we climb under and wade the stream and climb up the other side?"

"Of course, if you want to," Fred replied, "but it's hot, hard work and takes much longer."

"It isn't really so hard to walk across on the ties," said Larry. "I've done it once. They're only about a foot and a quarter apart. You don't get dizzy if you don't look through."

Paul and I tested out a few steps, and I looked through the ties to the stream that seemed far, far below.

"I think I'd sooner climb down and up the other side," I admitted, feeling giddy at the thought of going any farther. "Paul and I can go the slow way underneath, and you three can cross on top and wait for us. We won't keep you long."

"That's all right," said Fred and Mabel together, quick to relieve our embarrassment.

"I'm going with Paul and Eve," Larry said, in a tone that revealed he was really much happier about this.

We were impressed by the courage and skill with which Fred and Mabel took the crossing above our heads. Soon they looked like tiny toy figures up above on the trestle that supported the rails. We slipped and skidded down the steep, overgrown banks, getting scratched and dirty and covered with dust and perspiration.

But we made it down. Then we waded across the small stream. The water was clear and deliciously cool. We washed ourselves off, dried on our towels, and started up the other side.

"That was a waste of time," Larry teased. He was right. By the time we reached the top we were dirtier than ever.

Mabel and Fred looked so comfortably respectable and rested that we felt rather ashamed at having been afraid to walk over the viaduct.

"What would you have done if a train had suddenly come into sight?" asked Paul.

"Oh, it did one day when we were near the middle. We'd made a mistake on the time," said Fred. "We just climbed through to the supports beneath. It wasn't too hard."

"And the train went right over you!" I marveled.

"It shook the bridge terribly, Eve," Mabel admitted. "It was pretty frightening. But I borrowed Mother's watch today, so we can't make that mistake again."

"Will you cross on top on the way home?" Larry asked. "I will if you do, Paul."

"Maybe," Paul replied noncommittally. I said nothing at all. I hated to admit it, but the very thought frightened me. I was especially worried now by the thought of a train approaching when we were at mid-viaduct.

We walked on up the rails for half a mile, talking as we went.

"Here's where we leave the railway," said Fred. We were not certain what landmark showed that this was the place, but sure enough, when we crossed to the side of the embankment, there was a rough path through the scrub. We could see the tops of green trees in a valley nearby.

The path took us quickly to the top of a steep valley that was an almost vertical cut into the hills.

We helped each other down the bank, which had rough steps cut into it. They were slippery and moist. Clearly, underground water was seeping into this gorge. The five of us sidled down, landing at the base more or less in a heap.

What a scene lay before us! There was a rough, narrow path up the side of the stream that danced along in a series of tiny falls and rapids down the narrow gorge. The almost vertical banks were laced with maidenhair and kidney ferns growing among the soft mosses. Shafts of sunlight filtered down into the cleft through a few trees that clung to the rocky walls. Some dead trees had fallen across the canyon to form natural bridges with hanging gardens of ferns and creepers and spear-leaved bushes. The flickering sunlight turned each leaf it touched into a sparkling jewel.

"Just below us the creek plunges into a hole and goes underground for a way," Fred told us.

At each bend the canyon seemed lovelier than at the last. Then suddenly we came upon what to us seemed fairyland itself—paradise! We had been excitedly anticipating something of the kind from the increasing noise of falling water, but our hopes fell short of the reality.

From high above our heads where trees grew on the canyon rim, the stream leaped down onto an enormous moss-covered boulder that half filled the canyon itself. Over this slippery, mossy rock the water sprayed out and plunged again, down to a deep, clear pool at our feet, wide enough for good swimming and fringed with moss and ferns. The spray, and the sunlight filtering down through leaves, formed a double rainbow over the falls.

Paul and I stood there in speechless delight, but soon Fred and Mabel and Larry appeared, already in their bathing suits.

"Hurry up, you two slowpokes," Mabel called as the three of them scrambled along the canyon wall to the great rock that was the start of the second waterfall. They edged their way to where they could swing themselves out in a sitting posture on the rock in the full center of the fall. Swoosh, over its slope they went in a rushing, breathless slide and, with a plunge, down into the pool. They swam "ashore," and up they climbed again for the next slide.

Before long Paul and I joined them. We sat for a long time trying to get up courage for that first slide. Again and again we half started into the icy current and pulled back. The Lambeths did not tease or urge us, but left us to take our time.

Paul was the first to make it. He went down with a blood-curdling yell, which ended in spluttering bubbles in the pool. I could not let my younger brother beat me, so for sheer self-respect I let myself go. The few seconds before I hit the water were the longest I had ever known. On the way I badly wanted to reverse directions, but when I came up glowing and successful, I was as eager as the rest to do it again. We slid down, over and over, till we were all completely exhausted.

‖≡‖

"About time for lunch," Mabel suggested, for all three of the boys had begun to get chattering teeth and goose pimples.

"Girls have more fat on them," said Fred when Mabel and I teased them. We dried ourselves off, got back into our clothes, and then found a log where some sunshine reached us. The lunches, which had seemed so bulky and heavy to carry, disappeared in short order. Water from the fall was a delicious drink, bubbly fresh and clear and with a touch of the flavor of soil and ferns.

"Goodness! It's time we started back," said Mabel, checking the watch. "Cows won't wait."

CHAPTER EIGHT

We Become Celebrities

It was still two full hours till train time when we came to the viaduct.

"Well, how about it, you two?" asked Fred. "Are you going to walk across? Mabel and I will each keep step with one of you if you'll try it—you'll get all muddy again if you don't."

We felt ashamed to refuse, and we were so muscle-weary with our sliding, swimming, and scrambling up to the falls that it did look good to cross on the level.

"Let's go!" Paul and I agreed. Fred took my hand and Mabel took Paul's because, as Fred said, Paul was smaller, so it would be easier for Mabel to control his weight than mine if there were a stumble.

"Don't look through and don't look down," said Larry. "Just watch your feet, and every once in a while look ahead—that's the way I do it."

He was getting quite good at it as he made his way all alone for the first time; before, Fred had helped him as he was now helping me. When I was able to take my concentration off myself, I looked at Larry and thought his face was strained. He was finding it hard to behave as a big boy and keep going with no assuring older hand in his. Fred must have noticed the same thing, and perhaps Mabel did, too.

"We're almost halfway," she called encouragingly.

"I suggest we sit down for a few minutes," Fred said. "There's no great hurry because we've nearly two hours till train time. Let's dangle our feet and have a rest."

We sat there on the ties, huddled close together for security, our legs hanging down. From that sitting position it was fun to look at the stream far below us. The touch of dizziness it gave us from a resting posture was more thrilling than frightening.

"I like to look at the little creek and think it's ours," I said, "and that we know how it tumbles through the gorge and then disappears into the ground and comes up again."

"Are there any trout in it?" asked Paul.

"Young ones, down there," said Larry, "but not up in Paradise Valley. We did see some cock-a-bully fish in the pool under the falls."

"Well, time to get going again," Mabel reminded us.

Our minds had been free of the careful tie-stepping for those few minutes. Now, as we scrambled to our feet again, we felt less tense and greatly refreshed. We would soon be across. We resumed formation, Fred and I bringing up the rear.

Then it happened: the nightmare thing that I had feared!

"P-o-o-p! P-o-o-p! P-o-o-p!" went the awful whistle of a train! We all looked behind us, and there it was, bearing down upon us with one glaring eye. For what must have been a small part of a second, though it seemed an age, I was paralyzed. We all just stood there.

"P-o-o-p! P-o-o-p! P-o-o-p!" It screamed at us again, and

again and again. We knew we had been seen, out there on the viaduct. But a train cannot stop suddenly, as we well knew.

"Quick, don't panic," cried Fred calmly, taking charge. He and Mabel had already started to slip down between the ties to the great strut beams below. Larry was trying to do the same.

Fred reached up and grasped my hand firmly—he had left me standing there as he started to get his own position settled.

"Slip your leg down," he commanded. "I'll guide your foot to a strut. There—now the other foot." I trusted him and found myself perched.

Mabel was giving the same help to Paul. It was a perilous operation. Fortunately, all the Lambeth children could climb like monkeys. Fred and Mabel supported us firmly. Larry was making it on his own.

It seemed to take a long effort, but actually we must have made that climb down in mere seconds. We were all down now, nesting like strange birds on the supports of the viaduct, though we could still poke our heads up above the level of the ties.

The train, meanwhile, was bearing down on us like a monster, its searchlight shining even though it was daylight. It was getting huger every moment, still screaming its whistle and screeching its brakes. Since we had been seen, the engineer was trying to stop the train, and now it was actually slowing.

We poked our heads up and saw that it was indeed stopping. It might even be able to come to a halt before it was actually on the viaduct. So we stayed where we were and watched with fascination.

The reason it could stop so suddenly, we realized, was

that it was a very short train. It had only the engine, two passenger cars, and a baggage car.

Now the engineer and the conductor were getting out, looking very angry and worried and red in the face. There was a crowd of people, too, and some photographers taking pictures. They all seemed to be shouting at us at once.

"What are you kids doing on the viaduct?" the engineer called. "Trying to get yourselves killed?"

A thick-set, bald man pushed to the front, and everyone else stepped back respectfully.

"Bring them here," he said.

Some of the men, including the conductor, came out and helped us to complete our scrambling up. We were brought back across the viaduct, frightened and shamefaced, before this man whom we could see was some person of importance.

"This gentleman," said the conductor, "is the Prime Minister. Do you know you are making his special train late?"

"What are your names, children?" the Prime Minister asked us.

We all mumbled them.

"Are you going to the next station?"

"We are, sir," said Paul and I.

"Where are you others going?"

"To our farm, sir, just over there."

"Where have you been?"

We looked at the Lambeths, and they looked at us. We were remembering our oath.

"We're sorry, but we can't tell you, sir," I said.

"Oh yes, sir, we can. It is our secret, and we can," chorused Fred, Mabel, and Larry. We could see that

II≡II≡II≡II≡II≡II≡II≡II≡II≡II≡II≡II≡II≡II≡II≡II≡II≡II≡II≡II≡II≡III

we were released from our oath, so we all started talking at once about Paradise Valley.

The photographers asked us to pose with the Prime Minister and the Member for the District, and they took several pictures of us.

The Prime Minister and his party in this special train were on their way to open a new hydroelectric dam near Rotorua. There was to be a general election quite soon, and I suppose this made a story: "Prime Minister and party rescue children on railway viaduct."

The Prime Minister called his secretary. "See that there's a notice put up at both ends of this viaduct: 'Pedestrian crossing is forbidden on this bridge.'" Then, grinning at us, he said, "I'd like to see your valley sometime. Now, you two get aboard the train, and your friends, too, till we cross this bridge."

We waved good-bye to the Lambeths as they left the train on the other side. Paul and I rode in state to Tahitahi station in the Prime Minister's car. Everyone aboard waved to us as we climbed down to the platform. The few people at the station stared at us in wonder, especially the stationmaster. We offered no explanation at all and hurried home.

Next day our pictures were on the front page of the newspapers, and for a few days we were celebrities to everyone but our parents.

"Never do a stupid, dangerous thing like that again," said Dad. "Thank God you're still alive!"

||≡||≡||≡||≡||≡||≡||≡||≡||≡||≡||≡||≡||≡||≡||≡||≡||≡||≡||≡||≡||≡||≡|||

CHAPTER NINE

The Bull of the Swamps

In the early mornings, long before breakfast, at the right time of the year, Paul and I would go out in the pastures gathering mushrooms. "Full baskets, both," our parents would call as we tiptoed past their bedroom door. It was a wonderful feeling in the dewy grass, or after rain, to watch for the catch of light on the rounded white mushroom, newly pushed up out of the rich, crumbling earth. We would gently loosen it with two fingers, palm up, and lay it upside down in the basket, seeing the soft, pink gills of the young mushroom where the protecting sheath was pulling free of the stalk, or the rich bronzes and browns of the more mature mushroom gills.

Each of us would try to find more than the other—one of many kinds of natural treasure hunts we played. Some of the children gathered mushrooms for sale, but our family enjoyed eating them too much for that. We fried them in butter for breakfast when we returned home. We made them into milk and mushroom broth or mushroom omelettes for lunch, and we served them cooked many ways with meat for the evening meal.

We always kept a weather eye open for a bull in the

pasture and stayed close enough to a fence as a general precaution so that we could make an escape in an emergency. Twice a bull charged us, but each time we were safely outside the fence before the great animal pulled up snorting. Our precious mushrooms were strewn in the grass the second time, and we watched the angry bull trampling and pawing them.

Second only to the bulls as a danger in our valley was the river. It snaked around through steep banks, its deep green waters swirling and eddying in dangerous currents. But just as the mushrooms drew us into the pastures and close to the perils of the bulls, so the pleasures that lay along the riverbank lured us there.

One day in early spring, around the first of October, Paul gave me a fright. He and I had strolled down to the river at a point where we knew there were clematis vines climbing up the willows. The treetops were gay with great clusters of these gleaming white blooms, one of the most beautiful native flowers of New Zealand. I had taken a long pole with me to tease down the blossom clusters from the highest willow branches.

I was collecting these flower trophies for Mother, who loved the *pikiariro*—we called it by its Maori name, "the Lady of October"—but Paul was not very interested. He wandered off down the riverbank by himself to where he heard voices. A group of Maori children—two boys from Paul's class at school as well as Rangi, Pari, little Ruti, and a big boy called Honi who habitually teased Paul and me —were playing one of their traditional games. The would grasp a branch of the great overhanging willow, take a strong running jump out over the river, and drop off into the stream. Then they would swim to the nearest bend, where the current swept close to the shore, climb out, and be ready to take their turn doing it all over again. Almost all Maori children are strong swimmers, for they learn to swim even before they learn to walk. So they meant no harm when they called out to Paul, "Come on, Paul, show us you can do it, too!"

Paul stood irresolute. He must have known it was a risky thing to do with his limited swimming ability, but the desire to take the dare was strong. He slipped off his top garments and sandals as he replied, "Of course I can do it, too."

Wearing his shorts, he grasped the willow and swung well out, dropping down into the strong current of dirty-looking green water. Soon he was swimming desperately but floundering; he knew he could not make the bank at the bend as the others had done. The first I knew of it was when Rangi shouted wildly, "Eve, Eve, come and help Paul."

All the Maori children were streaking as fast as they could to the next bend, farther down the stream. I raced after them, the long pole in my hands.

But I had not counted on our Maori friends. Long before I made the bend, Honi had dived into the water at that point, followed by Rangi and Pari. They were waiting there to catch Paul as the stream swirled him around. Then the girls left him to Honi. Swiftly and skillfully he drew Paul to the bank and helped him out. They were not even alarmed by the incident.

"My goodness!" I panted. "You were crazy, Paul, to jump in there. You know you don't swim well enough for that." I felt really annoyed with him because of the scare he had given me.

"That's the best way to learn," Honi said with a grin. Then he said to Paul, "You're a spunky one. Come along with us another day, Paul. We'll soon teach you to swim and dive like a Maori."

"I think you were brave to jump in when you don't swim well yet," said little Ruti in a soft voice, and I could see that Paul, thoroughly flattered, was not repentant at all. He was in no mood to be attentive to a scolding from an older sister.

We had another wild experience shortly after this exploit of Paul's. It had nothing to do with mushrooming or with our dangerous stream, but it did involve a bull—or so we believed. It came about as a result of a sudden change in our way of life.

One evening we were doing our homework in a room next to the one where our parents were talking. We did not mean to listen, but they began to raise their voices.

"Martin, did I see you giving goods on credit today to Pita Tawa?" asked Mother.

"Oh, Alice, it was something I just had to do," said Dad. "He was getting food for the *tangi* of old Chief Kahunui. He says the old man died yesterday. How could I say no?"

"I wouldn't be surprised if there's no death and no *tangi* at all!" said Mother.

A *tangi* is a Maori funeral. All the kinsfolk from far and near come together for speeches and ceremonies at the carved meeting house, which is the center of each Maori village. It is a happy-sad time of feasting and dancing that goes on for days, and great quantities of food are eaten.

"It's not just Pita," Mother continued. "If we kept this a cash business, it would be smaller, and we wouldn't have to work so hard. And there would be security for me and the children."

Dad replied, "The people of this valley depend on our giving them aid when they need it, and faith when they would otherwise give up."

"It's no way to run a business," replied Mother, "especially in Tahitahi."

"I think Dad is right," I said.

"You would!" exclaimed Paul. "I'm with Mother. She's sharp."

The next evening, under the same circumstances, we overheard an even more disquieting conversation. It began in a way that made us nearly roll with laughter.

"I hate to admit it, Alice," Dad said, "but you were right about Pita Tawa and the *tangi*. There wasn't any. Old Chief Kahunui came walking into the shop when you were out getting dinner. He's hale and well, and there's no *tangi* for anyone. That crook Pita really put it over on me."

Mother laughed. And I, in the adjoining room, instead of feeling sorry for Dad, could not help indulging in some secret satisfaction that he, too, had been taken in by Pita Tawa's plausible roguery.

"You've got plenty of company in being deceived by Pita!" Mother continued. "But while we're alone, there's something I want to discuss. I'm not satisfied with what the children are learning at the Tahitahi school. One teacher for three classes isn't good enough."

"What do you suggest?" Dad asked.

"I think we should send them to the Rotorua school," she replied.

"How would they get there and back?" Dad questioned. "There are no trains at the right times."

‖≡‖

"David might take them in when he goes to work," Mother went on. We could tell she had it all worked out in her mind. "Perhaps Millie would let Alan go, too."

"They're happy at school here in Tahitahi, Alice," Dad interjected, "and anyway, how would they get home again?"

"They can walk home; it will be good for them," she replied. "They spend far too much time hunched up over their books."

"Alice, do you realize how many steps there are in five miles?"

"Martin, you never take the children's schooling seriously enough," Mother said. Then irritation mounted in her voice. "You grew up in the streets of Wellington without any father or mother and had no schooling after you were ten years old. No wonder you don't worry about the children's schooling."

"You're exaggerating the importance of schooling, Alice, just because you couldn't go on as far as you wanted with your own. You could have gone to high school and college if your father hadn't gone off fortune-hunting to the Australian gold fields and left your mother to cope with six children."

"Well," said Mother, "I want the children to have something better than the Tahitahi school!"

Our hearts thudded with apprehension, for Mother's voice seemed to carry a tone of finality. And so it did. Arrangements were made almost at once to send us to the Rotorua school.

This was still early October. I was nearing the end of fourth standard—sixth grade—since the school year begins in February in New Zealand, and Paul was in second standard—fourth grade.

 II≡II≡II≡II≡II≡II≡II≡II≡II≡II≡II≡II≡II≡II≡II≡II≡II≡II≡II≡II≡III

"Uncle David," I asked one morning, as we drove to Rotorua, "has Dad ever told you about his life when he was a child?" It was strange that I should feel free to ask him when I did not like to ask my father himself. Uncle David was the one adult from whom we kept almost no secrets.

"No," he replied. "As a matter of fact, I don't think anybody around here knows about your dad before he came to Tahitahi. Has he told you about it?"

"No, but we overheard Mother saying something that made us curious," I replied.

"Then why don't you ask him?" queried Uncle David.

"Well, we shouldn't have been listening in on Mother and Dad," Paul tried to explain as I sat feeling awkward and hardly knowing myself why I felt shy about asking Dad.

"You know," said Uncle David, answering what I had not put into words, "folks around here feel your dad is a kind of mystery man. Where does he come by all the things he knows and all the skills, they wonder. We know some of your mother's people. But Martin King's, no!"

Paul and I exchanged glances. So Dad was a mystery man. We loved mysteries.

"You know," continued Uncle David, "I think your father would tell you if you asked him."

"Maybe we will," I said.

"There's a saying," said Uncle David, " 'The lone hunter brings in the big game.' If you two really want to get your pop's story of when he was a boy, I think you should settle on one of you as the lone hunter. And I suggest Eve because papas are often soft on their girls, just like some mamas are on their boys, eh, Alan and Paul? How about Eve's stalking this big game? Someday when he's alone, you could get to helping him and just start in asking questions."

We liked that idea.

"Will you tell us what he says to you?" asked Alan.

"I'll tell Paul," I replied. "I don't know if I'll tell anyone else."

"Good girl!" said Uncle David.

"Good-bye, Uncle David," we called as we left him at the entrance to the school grounds.

The day passed slowly, but at last the three of us got together for the long walk home.

"How did it go today?" asked Alan. Lean, tall, and blond and in the sixth standard—two ahead of me—Alan was old enough to take the new school in his stride, as Paul and I were not.

"Horrid!" I exclaimed. "The kids called me a country bumpkin. The teacher got mad at me for mistakes in long division, and everyone laughed at me because when the history teacher asked me, 'Who was Henry V?' I replied, 'A character in Shakespeare.' He was, too!"

"I have a good teacher," said Paul, "and she's pretty. But most of the time I just don't know what the class is trying to do. I wish we could go back to the Tahitahi school."

We stopped and played for a time as we were passing Chinemutu, the Maori village by the lake, where there were many hot springs and the gutter ran with pleasant hot water. Here we took off our shoes and splashed around.

"Come swimming with us," some Maori children we had come to know at school called out to us. But we were still cautious about hot pools among the scrub and beside the lake, though we knew that the Maori people had used them for cooking and bathing for hundreds of years.

‖≡‖

"Some other day," I said, not wanting to hurt their feelings. "We're late this afternoon."

We passed a plantation belt of acacia trees in their golden puff balls of bloom, smelling delightful. We had to hurry Alan past this point or he would have lingered too long bird-nesting.

From there, along the flat land on the Rotorua side of our mountain, the road was built up across a swamp for about two miles. On either side were bulrushes and clumps of *toi-toi* grass, much like pampas grass, in full tassel. In places water gleamed, but mainly it was a treacherous bog, the home of many wild birds that were safe here from humans. We kept strictly to the road.

Suddenly a low roar filled the air. It echoed through the ground of the road we were walking on and seemed to set the earth trembling.

"A bull—run!" I cried, and I caught Paul's hand, sprinting at top speed. Alan grabbed his other hand, and we pulled him along, almost through the air, it seemed.

"I can't see it anywhere," Alan said as we slowed down.

"I can run by myself as fast as you're pulling me!" panted poor Paul, whose arms must have been almost loosened from their sockets.

"B-o-o-m! B-o-o-m!" It came again, that mysterious roar that seemed unearthly and evil. The terrifying thing was that the sound seemed to be all around us, so that we could not tell from which direction it came or where we should run. We just kept running in the direction of home, and our lungs seemed ready to burst. Each time we slowed down, however, that awful roar, like nothing we had ever heard before, shook the earth around us and set us running again.

We seemed to make those two miles across the swampy

stretch at an incredible pace. Then the road rose up out of the flats by Fairy Springs. This is a spot back from the road, on the side of Tahitahi Mountain, where a small stream gushes up from the earth full-grown through rainbow-colored sands. It has been stocked with rainbow trout, which swim around in their pretty stream-head, protected by the law.

We ran up the side road to the small cottage of the caretaker who had charge of this tourist attraction.

"A bull is after us," Alan gasped.

"You poor dears"—the old lady laughed—"don't you know what them things are?"

We shook our heads, too breathless for words.

"Them are bitterns—just big swamp birds. Around now, at mating time, the males put their heads down in the mud and let out that big, bellowing noise. The sound sort of gets bigger-seeming by echoing through the swamp. Keep me awake at night, they do, even though I should be used to 'em by now."

"To be scared by a bird!" said Alan, disgusted with himself.

"You're not the only ones," the kind old woman said. "We've had grown men run up here scared out of their wits." We still felt very foolish.

"Come inside," she said. "You're all done in." We surely were. "I'll get my Bill to drive you the rest o' the way home. I could do with some things from the store anyway."

That evening Dad and Mother decided this was the end of trying to send us to the Rotorua school. They were in complete agreement about it. We were a happy threesome next day, Alan, Paul, and I, when we went back to the familiar Tahitahi school and to all our good friends there.

More than ever my brother and I agreed we never wanted to leave Tahitahi.

Not long after that, Aunt Millie returned to her home town of Dunedin, on New Zealand's South Island, and Alan was enrolled in a boys' boarding school there.

CHAPTER TEN

Big-Game Hunting

Paul and I did not forget our curiosity concerning Dad, the mystery man.

"When are you going big-game hunting, Eve?" Paul asked.

But I bided my time as a hunter should. My chance came one afternoon. I was helping on a carpentry job. From babyhood I had found the smell of new-cut wood exciting. I had played endlessly with the shavings from Dad's plane, the sawdust that piled up under the sawhorse, and the discarded planks and blocks. By now I had learned to be useful.

"Dad," I asked, "what were you like when you were a boy? I've been wondering."

"Funny girl! You know, I never watched myself!" he replied with a grin.

He had been marking precisely where he meant to cut a heavy board. He reached for his well-greased and sharpened saw, and as his arm rose and fell, the saw bit steadily through the wood, giving off a rain of sawdust and making a rhythmic snore that seemed like a heavy intake and outlet of breath. I steadied the end of the board so its weight would not seize the saw or splinter the wood as the cut neared completion.

"Oh, tell me something you can remember," I wheedled.

"Why do you want to know, Eve?" he asked. I was getting nowhere. Suddenly I decided on a bold tactic, the direct approach.

I laughed. "Everybody wants to know, Dad," I said. "Do you realize you're a mystery man?"

Dad laid down his tool and stood looking at me a moment, astonishment on his face. Then he threw back his head and laughed aloud. "So!" he said, wrinkles of amusement still around his eyes. "Just because I keep my own counsel I've become a mystery man, have I?" He laughed aloud again. Then he added, more seriously, "There's no reason you shouldn't know all about me, or anyone else who wants to know, for that matter."

"Oh, Dad, I'm glad you're going to tell me," I said. "I really do want to know."

For a few minutes Dad just stood there, thinking.

"I can remember coming to New Zealand from England on a ship," he began. "I was with my parents, and my older brother, Charles, who was eight at the time. I was just 'little Marty,' a nipper of four," he continued.

"The main thing I remember from the voyage is falling down the companionway and getting burned in the engine room on one of the big furnace doors. The engineers petted and spoiled me after that, and they would bring me pieces of their helpings of plum pudding after dinner.

"I think I remember, even before that, when we lived with my grandparents in a large house with trees and fields. My father told me about it, anyway," Dad continued, "so I can't be certain that it is a true memory. It was in Somerset near the town of Bath. I do seem to recall seeing

llΞlllΞlllΞlllΞlllΞlllΞlllΞlllΞlllΞlllΞlllΞlllΞlllΞlllΞlllΞlllΞlllΞlllΞlll

my grandfather at a desk writing on paper with a printed picture on top, so I always liked to think that maybe it was a crest or coat of arms."

I tried again to bring him to the point Paul and I were so curious about. "Where did you live when you got to New Zealand?" I asked.

"We had a farm in the Hutt Valley, near Wellington, until I was ten years old," he said. "My father built our house, with help from some neighbors.

"He thought from the maps and plans we saw in England that the land he bought before he left there was in a village with churches and shops and a school. When we got there, we found it was just a hunk of wilderness.

"The house wasn't much, but he made a huge brick and homemade tile fireplace, and I remember he said, 'Someday I shall build our real home around this.'"

"Dad must be like his father," I thought, though I did not say it. "King's Folly" was what Tahitahi people called the touches of grandeur Dad worked into everything he made.

"What happened when you were ten?" I asked. At last I had my big game cornered.

"My brother and two sisters and I were left orphans," said Dad. "My mother died when my second sister was born. Our poor father told us, 'I am arranging for all of you children to go back to England to your grandparents. Granddad will be sending the fare. I shall join you later.'"

Then, after a pause, Dad added, "The next day my father rode out on the hills hunting for the wild pigs that were our main meat. He was found and brought home dead from a bullet wound. 'Accidental death' it was called at the inquest."

"Oh, Dad!" There were tears in my eyes as I thought of

those children in a strange land with no mother, and now no father, either. "What happened to you all?"

"Our two baby sisters were adopted by two different Wellington families. But no one wanted Charles or me. There were many strangers in the house, and we listened to them from behind our bedroom door. We heard the man who seemed to be the most important say, 'The two boys will undoubtedly have to be sent to an orphanage.'

" 'Come,' Charles then whispered to me. 'Let's escape. We'll run away. We won't go to an orphanage. Granddad will soon be sending for us.' So we just ran away."

"Wherever did you go, Dad?" This was better to me than any story in a book.

They had hidden in the bush, Dad told me, and then had made their way to the busy port city of Wellington.

"We forgot," said Dad, "that our grandfather now would be unable to get in touch with us. We kept out of the way of the police, and many people were kind to us. There was a hotel cook I especially remember, a great, fat, red-headed woman who let us do odd jobs for her. In return she allowed us to sleep in a shed in back of the hotel and to eat all the leftovers from the tables.

"There were hard times, that first winter especially," Dad told me. They had to put newspaper and cardboard in their shoes to cover the holes. The Salvation Army supplied them with warm overcoats. There were many other waifs getting along as best they could in the city, so they did not seem strange to people. Finally, Charles, who was a big boy for his years, pretended he was older than he was and found a good, steady job. Then things got better.

"What did you do, Dad?"

"After a while I became a delivery boy for a chemist, a

‖≣‖

good man who was very kind. He got me a bicycle to use for my work, and some new clothes and shoes."

"How did you learn so much when you didn't go to school?" I asked. To me, Dad seemed to know everything.

"The chemist let me act as night watchman at the shop. I had a bunk and slept there. There were rows and rows of books on his shelves, so at night I would read for hours. I found there are books to tell you almost anything you want to know. Afterward I learned to use the public library."

"Did your grandfather ever find you?" I asked.

"We were afraid even to inquire at the post office for a long time for fear we would be caught and taken to the orphanage," Dad replied. "Then Charles and I decided to tell the good chemist all about it. He made inquiries everywhere he could think of but turned up no news."

"Did you ever find your sisters?" I asked.

"It's funny that we didn't think of doing that till Charles was almost grown up," Dad confessed. "I'm sure we didn't tell the chemist about them. But we still remembered the name of one of the families who had adopted our younger sister. So one day, when I was about fourteen, we found out where this family lived and went to visit. Through them we found our other sister as well. Of course, the girls didn't recognize us, but they had been told that we were lost boys. They then told us how our grandfather had written and tried to find us and how he had eventually given up. They gave us Granddad's address and begged us to write.

" 'We don't want to go to England now, do we?' asked Charles that night as we strolled together on Lambton Quay.

" 'I guess not,' I replied. 'Not just now anyway. We're

getting along all right.' Then I added, 'And we're New Zealanders.'

" 'That's exactly how I feel,' exclaimed Charles. So we never did try to get in touch with our grandfather for fear he would pressure us to go to England.

"When I was nearly grown up—about eighteen, I think, but we never celebrated birthdays, so it's hard to be sure —I was working as a clerk at Kirkaldie and Stains Department Store in Wellington. One of my friends there got me to join a church he belonged to, and soon I made friends. One family asked me home for dinner. It was a pleasant, warm place—the first real home in which I'd had a meal in all those years since we became orphans. These people decided they wanted to send me to their mission college to become a medical worker. I deeply wanted to help the Maori people. I had Maori friends who had come to the port to work as stevedores, and they had told me how white doctors would seldom bother with the Maori folk in the distant villages when they were sick. And at the college I met Mother."

"Was she learning to be a medical worker, too?" I asked.

"Yes, and she was the prettiest and the smartest girl in the whole college," Dad told me.

"And you fell in love?" I asked eagerly.

"We fell in love, and we got married and came to work with the Maoris here in Tahitahi," Dad concluded, settling back to his carpentry.

I let out a big sigh. It was a satisfying story. Then I flung my arms around his neck. "I'm so sorry you didn't have a mother and daddy to love you all those years," I said.

"Come, let's not get carried away," Dad replied. "Dry

those tears. I'm here, and I've got two wonderful children, and I'm happy."

He lent me his large handkerchief to blow my nose. Like the Maoris whom he understood so well, Dad had a distaste for sentimentality. His feelings flowed easily, like the rivers of his native England. Both Paul and I were more like Mother in this respect, quick and intense, like the streams of her Scotland. I nestled in his arms, hampering the carpentry.

"I think you're wonderful," I told him.

"Tush!" he said with a laugh.

"Dad, isn't it strange that you and Pita Tawa both brought yourselves up?" Pita was much in my mind these days.

Dad looked surprised. He thought a moment. "Yes," he said, "I suppose we do have this in common."

"Not much else!" I laughed, thinking again about the *tangi* that wasn't. I hurried away to find Paul and tell him Dad's story.

‖≡‖‖≡‖‖

CHAPTER ELEVEN

"To the Four Kings"

At last Christmas week began. It was midsummer, and the long school vacation had already started. The weather had grown sunny and warm. Despite the summer heat, most New Zealanders think of snow at Christmas because they, or their parents, or their grandparents or great-grandparents, came from one of the countries of the Northern Hemisphere, where it is midwinter in December.

We helped our parents decorate the store windows with puffy balls of cotton—cotton-wool, we called it—which did look rather like snowflakes. We arranged a large Santa Claus in one window, too.

The store stayed gay and very busy the week before Christmas as we sold lots of toys and sweets, clothing and household goods. The help that Paul and I could give was welcome, and we had great fun trying to see that everyone found the right gift for the stocking he or she had in mind. Often Paul or I could come up with a good suggestion. We did not have much money to spend on gifts. For the most part we made our own gifts. They were more fun and much better than most of the things we could have bought. It took ingenuity to work on them, however, without the person for whom they were intended suspecting.

That Christmas, with help from Dad, I made Mother a padded footstool, upholstered with pieces of carpet left over from the living room floor. I finished it with braid trim and labeled it "For Mother's tired feet." With Mother's help, using the same carpeting and braid, I made Dad a handsome pair of slippers. And for Paul I made a fishing rod. Again Dad helped, so the reel worked, and the rod was strong and smooth.

Christmas Eve came at last. Our parents kept the store open till nearly midnight, but we confidently hung up our stockings, knowing that however late our parents went to bed, they would first fill our stockings to the bursting point. We made Dad and Mother hang up stockings, too, and filled these before we went up to bed ourselves. Besides our homemade gifts, often too large to fit inside the stockings, we bought little things for them from the rival store that had opened across the street two years before. We were careful that the fruit or candy or odds and ends on which we spent our pennies were of kinds not sold in our own store so that our parents would be surprised.

Christmas morning saw us downstairs early, poking around our stockings and packages, though we would not open anything until Mother and Dad were up. They must have been weary and sleepy, but they did not keep us waiting too long.

Tagged to the outside of Dad's stocking this Christmas morning was an envelope, and printed on it (so we would not know the writing, though of course we could recognize Dad's print, with its draftsman's perfection and regularity) in strong black letters were the words: "TO THE FOUR KINGS."

Paul and I were too intrigued by that envelope to begin to open our own gifts, tucked into the stockings in mysterious shapes.

〓〓〓〓〓〓〓〓〓〓〓〓〓〓〓〓〓〓〓〓〓〓〓〓〓〓〓〓〓

"Oh, Dad! Please open it first of all," we pleaded. Dad and Mother were both smiling mysteriously.

"I think you should, Martin," said Mother.

"Well, here goes," said Dad, drawing out the suspense almost unbearably by having all sorts of make-believe difficulties in getting the envelope unstuck. Finally, out fell a pair of keys. And a book. The book, which Paul grabbed, was an instruction manual for a Chevrolet!

"Does that mean . . ." began Paul, but he trailed off, unable to voice his wildest hope.

"Well, now," Dad said, "that probably explains something that was left last night in the horse paddock, all covered up with a sheet canvas. Slip on shoes and coats and we'll see."

"Oh, Daddy! Is it really a car?" asked Paul.

"Stop guessing," said Dad, trying to sound stern.

"What color is it?" I asked, hoping to make him betray whether it really was a car or not.

"Green," he said, falling into my snare.

By this time we had put on our shoes, and with our coats over our nightclothes we headed for the horse paddock at a run.

Sure enough, there it was—the draped outline of a car. Paul and I arrived together and quickly peeked under the canvas. Even this glimpse showed me it was a soft blue-gray, not green; but then Dad was color-blind.

"Step back now," called Dad as he and Mother arrived at a more sedate pace. "I'm doing the unveiling."

In one deft movement he whirled off the canvas cover. The new car stood revealed in all its splendor in the morning sunshine.

"Oh, it's beautiful." We feasted our eyes, and Paul studied the dashboard, gearshift, and brake. We could

hardly tear ourselves away from this glorious sight, but the rest of Christmas awaited us inside.

Paul had made me a model of the Wright Brothers' airplane that really flew when you pulled a launching string just right. Dad had made us a beautiful set of peg quoits. Mother had made the dress I wanted of all dresses and had been drawing in my notebooks for months. But lovely as all the other presents were, after the car they were tame pleasures.

Then New Year's Day came around, and we went to

Manurana Springs for a picnic. We had a wonderful time, and after dinner that evening we gathered around the organ while Mother played and Dad sang, and we two children joined in as best we could.

Afterward Dad said, "Mother has something very special to tell you."

"We're all going away for a holiday together, children, to the seaside, to Tauranga and the Mount. The arrangements are made. We've even rented a beach cottage."

For a moment Paul and I were struck speechless with delight, but then the thought of what would happen to the store suddenly brought me up short.

"Oh, Mother," I cried, "will we have to close the store?"

Mother smiled and said, "We've found a fine young man who'll manage the store for us the two weeks we'll be away. He's coming tomorrow, and we hope to be able to leave in four days."

We hugged Mother and Dad and danced around the room together in our excitement.

‖≡‖

CHAPTER TWELVE

Vacation by the Sea

Ted, the young assistant for the store, came the next day. He was kind and friendly, and we loved and trusted him at once. In a few days we were ready to leave.

The Chevy left heavily laden. We took many of our provisions for the two weeks, as well as bathing suits, balls, books, and paper. Dad laughingly said that our family uses up enough paper to support a small pulp mill! We all loved to doodle and draw and write.

We drove through trees much of the way to Tauranga, over range after range of bush-clad hills with deep gorges in between, down and up as the road snaked above steep cliffs. Here and there forest giants towered over the other trees; they stood as lonely, blackened skeletons in semi-clearings that had been burned over to make new farms. New trees were planted around the farm homes and fields, but these were the trees of England or Europe or America—willows and poplars and Monterey pines, cypress and redwoods, and, of course, fruit trees.

Paul and I could hardly wait for our first glimpse of Tauranga harbor and the Mount. We vied with one another as to who would see it first. Paul won—or at least he got in his shout ahead of mine.

Tauranga was a beautiful little town merging into orchards and rich farmlands. It lay between two arms of the sea—the shallow back bay, where people went flounder-spearing at night with lanterns reflecting in the ripples, and the main front harbor with its shops and long wharf. On the far side of the harbor, protecting it from the great rollers of the Pacific beating into the Bay of Plenty, hills flattened out into a peninsula of sand dunes. The hill ended, right at the harbor mouth, in a strange, small mountain called Mount Maunganui, or more often just the Mount. This was a favorite beach resort for people nearby, and the dunes cradled numbers of tiny cottages that could be rented. The harbor beach was safe and calm for swimming. The open ocean beach beyond offered splendid surfing, with mountainous breakers tumbling up the gently sloping sands.

As we drove into town, we knew that we would have to leave the Chevy at the wharf and go by a ferry launch. That was part of the excitement. The Mount had no place for a car, and there was no approach road to take one there. The launch chugged across; it was the largest vessel on which Paul and I had ever traveled.

We had to make several trips across the dunes to carry our baggage from the small landing wharf to our tiny two-room cottage, but soon we had moved everything.

"Can we go down to the beach now?" Paul asked eagerly as we dumped our last load.

"We'll help straighten up when we get back," I put in. We could hear the sound of the waves pounding on the beach, and we were sniffing that wonderful aroma of the open ocean.

"I really should stay and get things a bit shipshape," said Mother.

"Oh, come, Alice!" Dad exclaimed. "How can we make our royal salute to the ocean without the queen? We'll all pitch in together after we get back."

So Dad and Mother and Paul and I set out for the ocean beach. It was hard walking. Even on the paths we sank into the warm sand, but it felt delightful on our bare feet. We found new kinds of flowers and plants growing on the sandhills, and clumps of "cutty grass," which we avoided.

And then, there it lay—a sweep of giant waves shone and swirled in the bright sunshine and broke on the beach, rushing up to us in a foaming flood, then receding into the next wave, leaving the sands washed and clean and shining. The beach extended all the way to where we could see, opposing the waves, a jutting outcrop of rock called the blow hole. We were content for quite a time just to stand where the wash from the long waves bubbled over our feet and ran back, fascinated by the power and the rhythm of the curling breakers.

Over the wet sands flew sea gulls, so white themselves but reflecting on the sands as skimming black shadows. Tiny, quick-moving little sea birds darted about after small crabs in the sand.

"Well, are you ready to wet those bathing suits?" Dad asked.

"Brr!" exclaimed Mother at the thought of the ordeal of the cold water. "But I guess we all must make that salute to the ocean."

Our parents took us only to where the water was about their middles, but each madcap wave buffeted us about. The water was cold but exhilarating, and soon all of us glowed warm. We found that if we jumped just right, facing toward the shore and watching the approaching breaker over our shoulders, we could jump up, catch it, and

‖≡‖

float in on it. But often a wave broke over us, and we came up gasping and spluttering.

"Chalk one up to the ocean," Mother said, laughing.

At last, a little exhausted, we were very content, Paul and I, to go back to the sand. Mother soon joined us, and then Dad went for a real swim out beyond the breakers. We were all ready to do justice to the dinner we helped her to prepare after we got back to the cottage.

We went swimming in the ocean several times a day, and Dad swam in the quiet water on the harbor side of the Mount as well. Mother liked to collect shells along the beach even more, and often we joined her. We liked to pick up the large whorled shells and put the openings to our ears, listening to the murmur that seemed to echo the sea. We found interesting pieces of driftwood, too.

"We're going to have a full car on the trip home," Dad said as our collection mounted.

Often we hunted for rock mussels, large and black, with good, edible shellfish within; they were hard to dislodge from their hold on the rocks. We gathered *pipi*, tasty little shellfish like clams, but smoother and flatter of shell; they bury themselves down in the sand and breathe through air-bubble holes. We would dig them up and take them back to the cottage in our buckets. Plunged into boiling water, the mussels and *pipi* cooked quickly, and their shells opened. They made a fragrant, delicious feast with nothing else needed but bread and butter, and for our parents the inevitable cup of tea.

We walked around the steep cliffs on the seaward side of the Mount, careful to keep to the path. There were some great *pohutukawa* trees here, called the New Zealand Christmas tree because at this season it bears its load of vivid red powder-puff blossoms. Now, in January, some were still in bloom, and we brought boughs of them back to decorate the cottage. The trees were handsome themselves, with their wind-blown shapes and silvery-backed green leaves. Where these trees stood on gentle slopes, we would climb some of their lower limbs or swing from them. Mostly they leaned back against the slope of the hill or the cliff faces.

The four of us climbed all the way to the top of the Mount. Here there was always a wind, and the patterns of the ocean and land lay spread beneath us like a map.

One day as I was burying myself in the warm sand, I heard Dad say, "Alice, I've often marveled that you so readily agreed to my buying the car now, at a time when you've been worrying so about finances. Thank you, dear, for having the faith in me to let me do what I wanted. It has worked out well for us all, hasn't it?"

"Yes, indeed, Martin. I, too, was longing for this holiday, and the car helped to make it possible." Then she paused a moment and added, "I wish so much I could let you believe that it was just because I had faith in you, but in all honesty I've got to tell you there were other reasons as well."

"What reasons, Alice?"

"Many things just at this time," Mother said softly, "made me change my point of view. I decided not to think any more, or worry any more, about what I sense as danger ahead in the store, but to take it that whatever is to be is to be. Perhaps it is God's will that we are to leave Tahitahi and the store and go back into full mission work."

"Really, Alice, I believe my position in the store is quite sound. I own more than enough to cover all that I owe," Dad replied. I could tell he was just a little hurt.

"Martin, I've been thinking a great deal on this trip, and I want you to do one thing to relieve my mind and to reduce the danger, or at least what I feel may be danger."

"What is it, Alice?"

"You know how the road that runs up past the old mission house, now the fishing lodge, cuts our property in half. I want you to put all the property on the lodge side of the road in my name. Then if trouble came in the store business, no claim could be made on this."

"My shrewd little Scot," Dad smiled. "Yes, it's a good idea. We'll do it as soon as we go home. Also, I'll keep Ted on at the store, and I'll spend all the time I can building on your side. I want to put up two cottages there for rental, and another small store building on that corner. Tahitahi is growing fast, and buildings are needed. Your side isn't really as valuable now as mine is, but I'd like to make it so. It would be good rental income for you if anything should happen to me."

"And thank you for understanding this time," Mother said. Dad drew her to him.

I got up and ran to the beach. "I don't ever want to leave Tahitahi," I said to myself once again, "but Dad must be right. There's really nothing to worry about. Mother does let things worry her too easily."

CHAPTER THIRTEEN

The Rescue

Two days before our holiday was over, a great storm blew up. It was exciting to see the ocean in an angry mood. We had not imagined that the waves could get so huge. Spume blew in the air like dirty suds from a washtub, and the wind howled. Even the distance from our cottage to the beach became hard to walk, and the blowing sand stung our legs and faces. It was cold, too, as it can suddenly be at any season in New Zealand, even summer.

Then it rained, with thunder and lightning, flattening out the waves a little and driving us indoors. We read some of the books that we had neglected till then. The cottage roof leaked a good deal, and the windows and doors rattled.

"What gimcrack carpentry!" exclaimed Dad.

We hoped the cottage would not collapse and blow away. But we felt cozy there, all together, in the close space. The next morning it was still rainy and very cold, but the wind seemed to have died down considerably.

"Who's for joining me in a walk along the ocean beach to the blow hole this morning?" said Dad after breakfast. "The storm may have thrown up all manner of strange things, and the blow hole should be spouting high."

‖≡‖

Paul and I began scrambling into our raincoats almost before Dad had finished speaking. Mother said it was too cold and windy for her and that she would write some letters while we were gone.

The tide had come almost fully in, and the waves were still thundering high. They dashed farther up the beach than we had ever seen them before. As a result, we had to walk in the heavy sandhills. Though they were well dampened by the rain, they were not so easy to walk on as the flat, smooth, shining sands left solid by the retreating tide. But it was wonderful to be outdoors again.

We would really have more chance of finding interesting debris from the storm after this high tide had receded. Dad knew this, and so did we, but we wanted the walk.

The sand, under the driving wind, was starting to dry again and to blow with a sting against the backs of our legs—it helped us along so that we hardly realized what a long way we had walked, our backs to the Mount and the wind. We had nearly reached the blow hole. It was blowing like a geyser with each large wave. We passed the point on the beach where a notice said "DANGER. NO SURFING BEYOND THIS POINT: STRONG CROSSCURRENTS."

"I think this is as far as we should go," Dad said. "It's going to take us much longer to get home than it did to get here; we don't want to leave Mother alone too long."

Dad was right. Walking home against the wind, which had become stronger and colder than ever, was not easy.

Paul, who had very sharp eyesight, had been staring out to sea, watching the waves. "What's that, Dad?" he asked, pointing to something he thought he saw out in the turbulent water just beyond the line of breakers, about two hundred yards off shore.

‖≡‖

"It's the keel of an overturned lifeboat!" Dad exclaimed. "And there are men clinging to it." Even as he spoke, he was stripping to his underwear. Dad was a strong, though not a fast, swimmer. He paused a moment on the beach, calculating how best to attack the currents. He considered going out to the blow hole and swimming the longer distance from this slightly outjutting rock across to the overturned boat. But he decided against it and instead dived into that tumbling mess of waves and crosscurrents, which at this point were particularly bad, and was heading to the rescue through the chilly water. He did not swim directly into the currents, but rather tacked with them, making use of their tug and pull as he felt it, so that his course was a zigzag one.

Paul and I were terribly frightened. We expected at any moment to see Dad disappear and get swept away and out to sea. We stared, breathless.

"There he is! . . . There he is again!" we kept saying as he would disappear in a wave and then reappear.

Now he was approaching the boat at a sharp tangent. It would be tricky to avoid being struck by it as it tossed around in the waves. We could not even see for sure how many men still clung to it, for it moved around so. We were not certain that there were any, though we thought we caught sight of three heads as the boat tossed in the wave troughs.

"He's getting one man off now!" exclaimed Paul.

"He's struggling with Dad, the silly man!" I exclaimed angrily, knowing how dangerous this could be.

We saw Dad give him a quick blow that must have made the man unconscious.

"He's coming steadily now," said Paul.

‖≡‖

Before very long Dad's feet touched bottom, and we rushed to the edge of the water to help to pull him and his burden ashore.

It appeared he had rescued a seaman, judging from the man's clothes. Dad was bending over, panting, as he recovered from the hard swim. Then he quickly turned the man so that water would run out of his mouth, and he told us to start artificial respiration. He had taught us how to do this.

"Oh, Dad! You're not going back!" I exclaimed, alarmed.

"There are three men," Dad said, and he was off again into those terrible waves. Again he zigzagged toward his target, using the forces of the current.

But he had given us a job to do—not an easy one, either. Paul kept the man's mouth open and held his tongue out so he would not choke, while I used all the strength I had to force air out of and into his lungs. I knew of two ways to do this, and I alternated them every few minutes in the hope that I would be doing at least one of them well enough to bring him around. We did not know the method of breathing into the mouth, which would have been easier and more effective. But soon he did seem to be breathing, though he remained unconscious.

"That must have been quite a knock that Dad gave him," said Paul with a grin. "But he seems to be all right."

Then we turned our attention to Dad. He was at the overturned boat again and was watching his chance to grab one of the two remaining men. They must both have been so nearly exhausted with the cold and the strain of holding on in that buffeting sea that I could imagine that the one left behind this time might feel he had no chance of keeping his grip till Dad got back again—that is, if indeed Dad would have the strength to go back again. He would try, I knew, even if he lost his life doing it. That was Dad, and nothing we could say would stop him.

"That one's behaving better!" cried Paul. Dad did not need to waste any strength in knocking him unconscious, but the man was too weak to help himself, or perhaps could not swim. Dad was doing it all, and we could see that he was tiring. He was moving shoreward very slowly now. We went close to the dangerous water, both of us, and waited breathlessly.

"Give me your hand," I said to Paul as Dad and his burden got close. "Keep hold of it and pull when I get hold of Dad." I let the waves come up above my knees. Dad was moving very slowly now. I caught his hand, and Paul and I helped to pull him and the other man ashore. This time Dad lay on the sand, breathing in great gasps. He motioned us to get going on the second man he had rescued. He was very waterlogged, but I could still feel a slight pulse. Water ran out of his mouth as we worked on him, but in a few minutes we could hear him breathing in a gurgling, rattling way.

The first man was stirring to consciousness. Dad got up, looking very groggy.

"Oh, Dad, don't go. You just can't make it again," I protested.

"I believe I can," he said. Then he added sternly, "Don't come into the water again like that to help me. No matter what happens, don't come in. *That's a command!* These currents could catch you and whirl you under and away. Remember—*stay on the beach, no matter what happens.*" Then he added, "I'll be all right this time. I've got my second wind now, and the other man can swim a bit."

‖≡‖

He was off again. We left the two men lying there on the wet, windy sand, and stood at the edge of the water, following Dad's every move.

"The man's coming to meet him," Paul shouted. "He's left the boat and is trying to swim in himself."

The man was doing as Dad had done, swimming in zig-zags, using the currents. We were so relieved. This improved Dad's chances a lot, for we knew he was risking his life with each attempt, and this last trip most of all. But each time he was out of sight in a wave or was pulled off course by the undertow and the swirling crosscurrents, we held our breaths till our hearts seemed almost to stop beating.

The swimmer from the boat was not doing well, but at last Dad reached him. He was getting the man to rest a hand on his shoulder and to use one arm to swim and kick with his feet the way he had done with us when he was first teaching us not to be afraid of the water. They were doing well—much better than last time. This was easier than dragging a dead weight, and Dad certainly had his second wind. He was touching the bottom and supporting the all but exhausted man beside him sooner than we had hoped. Then they both struggled to where we stood and flopped over on the sand. At once we were hugging Dad in our relief.

"Back a bit, let me breathe," he said.

Then he looked around. "You two have a job ahead," he said when he regained his breath. "You'll have to go for help. It's going to be tough walking against the wind. Get Mother to find six men, and have them bring three stretchers with blankets and hot-water bottles—drinking water, too, and a bottle of brandy. Off you go, and don't come back. Get into warm clothes and stoke up the stove.

‖≡‖

I'll try to get a fire going here. I've a newspaper and matches in my coat pocket. Off now."

We started at a fast run, glad that we could help in the rescue. The heavy sand underfoot and the wind in our faces soon slowed us to a jog-trot, and before long we were just walking as fast as we could with our heads thrust forward against the wind and holding our jackets as much as we could over our faces. The sand stung them; our lips and noses felt blue and frozen with cold.

Every few minutes we would jog-trot again as long as we could manage it, till our lungs felt like bursting. We had to fight our way every step.

I was saying in my mind over and over all the things Dad wanted: "Six men, three stretchers, blankets, hot-water bottles, water to drink, and some brandy." I hoped I had it right. I said it twice aloud between gasps for breath so that Paul would help to check me.

"They must be off some boat wrecked in the storm," I said through teeth clenched against cold, so that my voice sounded strange.

"Let's hope Dad doesn't see any more survivors," gasped Paul.

It was selfish, but I hoped so, too. I didn't want anyone to drown, but better unknown people than Dad.

"We're nearly there," cheered Paul at last. "See, there's where the path starts down to the cottages."

It was true; we had nearly made it. With a burst of energy and confidence we started to run again and kept it up all the way to our cottage door.

"Mother, Mother," we burst in, scaring the wits out of her, "Dad's just swum out near the blow hole and rescued three sailors from drowning. They're all half dead, and

Dad's trying to make a fire. He says you're to hurry and get six men and three stretchers. While you do that, we'll get the other things he wants."

Mother wasted no time asking us questions, except two. "Is Dad all right? He's not going out again?"

"He's fine," I said. "There were just the three men, and he's brought them in."

Mother went quickly from one cottage to the next. Meanwhile, we piled together all the blankets we had in our cottage, built up the fire in the stove, and put up water in our stock of camp pots. We soon filled the hot-water bottles. (Dad despised such things, but the rest of us liked them on cool nights, even in summer.) We filled a cider bottle with drinking water and remembered to include a tin cup. We tied all these things in the sheet of canvas we used at picnics, then gave the bundle to Mother, who was assembling the relief party.

"Dad says to take the brandy," I told her.

"I was going to," she said, coming inside to get it.

"You don't need to go, Mrs. King," one of the men said.

"Of course I'll go," she answered.

We watched them from the window as they set out. It had not been hard to find six men among our fellow campers, for even the sturdiest fishermen among them had been driven indoors by the cold wind that morning. Army-style canvas and wood cots, which were what most of us had to sleep on, made good first-aid stretchers.

"They don't know what it's going to be like, beating back against that wind," Paul said as we admired the pace they were setting.

"Let's do what Dad said and get warm," I added.

Soon we had the kettle of water singing for tea, and a

‖☰‖‖

large pot of canned soup hot and ready to serve when the party returned. We watched from the window.

"There they are!" shouted Paul.

The three stretcher parties were way in advance, but behind them we could see Dad and Mother coming along together, helping one another.

All of them came straight to our cottage. Our hot soup was just what was needed, along with cups of steaming tea with lots of sugar and milk for all but Dad, who liked his plain.

The three sailors had perked up considerably by this time. Dad had gotten a fire going on the beach, and they had stayed warm on the trip back to the cottage. We found out that their ship had indeed sunk in the storm, and so far as we ever learned, they were the sole survivors. A launch soon came for them from Tauranga, and they were taken for a checkup in the hospital there.

By then, it was time for us to pack up for home.

The next day turned out beautiful and sunny, and on the drive back our parents detoured a little to show us Tauranga. "I'd like to come here to live someday," said Mother.

"I would, too," Dad replied.

Paul and I looked around carefully. Many of the streets out from the town were wide, tree-shaded lanes, where flowers, thrown out long ago from gardens, grew wild in the grass. There were arum and flag lilies, honeysuckle, forget-me-nots, periwinkles, irises, and climbing roses. Mother said there were daffodils and other bulbs along the roadsides earlier in the spring. We took an extra-hard look at the school and high school, which were together.

"Neat," said Paul. "We could be going to the same school

even for the two years when you'll be in high school ahead of me." We agreed it was the most attractive town we had seen.

"But it's good to be going home!" Paul said as we left Tauranga. The return trip slipped by quickly. The first glimpse of the lake—our lake—and of Mokoia Island sent our hearts thudding with delight.

‖≡‖

CHAPTER FOURTEEN

The Pony

The next year was a rather strange one for me. I was beginning to grow up, sometimes against my will, and I spent many of my spare hours helping in the store.

One day I was wrapping mutton birds. These are strong-smelling young nestling sea birds, killed and preserved in their own fat, as well as in oil, and packed in great casks. The Maori people consider them a great delicacy, but if care was not taken, the smell of them drove white customers out of the shop. It was Pita Tawa who was buying them today, and with cash.

He sat easily on the edge of the counter, his crutches beside him, as Mother gave me some help in quickly wrapping the mutton birds in many layers of paper and closing down and sealing the lid of the cask.

My feeling about the brooch had by now mellowed considerably.

"How's your pony?" I asked him. I could see Sheila hitched to the railing outside the store, and the sight of her always rekindled my desire for a pony of my own.

"Pony very good," said Pita. "You know," he continued, "this not the first horse I have. I ever tell you, Eve, 'bout my big black racehorse?"

"No, Pita." Here was another of his wild stories coming,

I felt sure. The other customers knew it, too, and moved closer. There were no Maoris among them; I had noticed that Pita was quieter when there were other Maoris around. He made himself even more comfortable, which I took to mean that it was a long story.

"One day I buy racehorse from old man Casey. You know old Casey farm? Why I buy him? Well, I go out to farm that day. Old man Casey very sad, broken-hearted sad. 'What for you sad?' I say. 'Oh, my big racehorse,' Casey say, 'name Black Keri, he win many race for me. Now he dead out there in the field. He die last night. No reason I see. Just dead.'

"I say to Casey, 'Cheer up. You sell Black Keri to me. Then you take money, go Rotorua, have one big drink, forget all trouble.' "

Pita's eyes caught and held mine as he talked. Did he intend a special message for me in the story?

"Casey say, 'What for you wanta buy dead racehorse?'

"I say to him, 'I like dead racehorse. Maybe I stuff like in museum.'

"So I pay Casey some money, he write receipt on paper: 'I sell Black Keri to Pita Tawa, this day this place!' Then he go to town, get roaring big drunk, many days." Pita paused to fill his pipe as we all hung onto his story, even Mother.

"I take paper and go village, say to Maori friends, 'See, Pita Tawa buy racehorse Black Keri. This paper prove it.'

"I say, 'But man with crutches no can ride so good. Black Keri too big, too wild. I get little slow horse. I raffle Black Keri. You give me five pound, put name in hat. Lucky man draw Black Keri.'

"So all them Maori give me five pound, put name in hat. We draw. Lucky man get name pick out of hat. He dance. He shout. He sing: 'I got Black Keri!'

‖≡‖

"All Maori then run all the way out to Casey farm see Black Keri. I go Post Office Savings Bank, put all money in bank but one five pound.

"Long time wait. Then big noise. Maori cry! Maori shout! 'Black Keri dead! Black Keri dead!' they say. They very angry Pita Tawa. 'You know Black Keri dead,' they say.

"I say, 'You, there, you man win Black Keri?' I hand him five pound. Then I say other Maori, 'You men no win Black Keri anyway. Why you mad Pita Tawa? You lose raffle anyway.' So Maori think, 'He right, too!' So all them Maori go away. Pita Tawa happy. Many pound in bankbook." Pita winked at me and picked up his package.

True or not, it was a good story, the old rascal!

Mother kept trying, all that year, to make me give up my tomboy ways, but I did not take readily to ladylike ideas. I frequently climbed on the back of our old plow horse. And I seemed somehow estranged to myself. The least thing upset me, and I felt oddly unhappy much of the time.

Paul now spent most of his days with his boy friends. Except for several good friends, like Mabel, I found other girls rather dull. To be fair, I think they found me dull, too. In fact, they had a way of shutting me off from their intimate conversations at school.

Mostly they were more mature than I was, and older. Bessie, in the class ahead of me—the sixth standard, or eighth grade—was almost sixteen. She left in the middle of the year to get married, and we all knew she was going to have a baby soon. Blanche, also in the senior class and almost sixteen, left in midyear as well, to marry a neighboring farmer.

In my own fifth standard (seventh grade), Rangi and Pari were already planning to become tourist guides at

Rotorua when they finished their senior year. They would be popular, I knew. During the day they would wear traditional Maori clothing—the colorful braided headband, with a *huia* feather in it, the swishing dance skirt over the bright cotton dress the missionaries introduced long ago, and for much of the time bare feet or sandals. They would charm the tourists and be paid to be photographed as they guided them around the hot pools and geysers. In the evening they would return to Rotorua town. They would get into smart, modern clothing and high-heeled shoes and have very happy times. It was a life somewhat beyond my understanding.

"Mother, I wish I had a pony," I said one day. I knew that our parents had been having serious business problems. That was why, up till then, I had kept my desire to myself.

"I wish we could get you one, Eve, but just now it isn't possible," Mother replied.

I never asked again. The year slipped away.

Several times during the summer vacation, around Christmas, Mabel rode down to our place with one of the Lambeth horses on a lead, saddled and bridled. We would go for long rides together.

Then, quite suddenly, near the middle of January, there came a strange turn in our family affairs that completely altered the pattern of life for Paul and me.

Our family came to own a farm. The way it happened was odd. For several years our parents had been trying to help two English brothers make a success of their farm, but it was not a good spread. Its thin coat of sandy soil was, as Dad said to Mother, "an excellent place to sink and lose a fortune." Dad and Mother had extended them a great deal of credit for seed, for fertilizer, and for machinery.

One January morning the two brothers came into the store and said, "Well, we're leaving you the farm and all that's on it. It should bring you some of your money back, though not all, after the mortgage is paid."

"Where are you going?" asked Mother.

"Home to England," one of the brothers said. "Our parents have sent our fares, and they want to start us in something else—anything else will do us, so long as it isn't farming."

"About the last thing we need just now," said Dad, "is a farm—and especially *that* farm." But we needed to get back all of the debt we could, and luckily this was a rather slack season at the store as well as our long vacation. So once more Ted, the young assistant, took over the store completely for a time, and with a great bustle of packing, we were off to "our farm."

Most of the land had been cleared, though there were bush-clad hills all around. The farmhouse was unpainted frame. It looked lonely, with no plantings of trees immediately around it and with an odd pinnacle of rock rising quite sharply, like a small mountain, not far from the back door.

"Let's run up that strange hill at the back of the house, Eve," said Paul as we were unpacking our goods in the farmhouse.

There were only two bedrooms in the house. "We're going to have to build a third," said Dad, "and meanwhile we'll partition off part of the kitchen as a bedroom for you, Paul. And this summer vacation you two can help me paint the house, and then in the next few months we'll get some young trees started around it."

"That'll be fine, Dad," Paul replied, his mind on the hill

at the back. We disappeared outside. We couldn't wait another minute to climb it.

We scrambled up through the bracken that grew wherever it could get a foothold in the rock.

"What shall we call it, Paul?" I pondered as we
climbed.

"Maungatiti," suggested Paul. "Little Mountain."

"Our little mountain," I said softly as we perched on the
summit, surveying our new kingdom. There were the usual
farm buildings, horse paddocks and pigpens, a good water
supply from a small stream, and some large, fenced grassy
fields where about a dozen cows were grazing. Behind the
fields, between them and the bush, was wild scrub country
that we loved, very hilly and intriguing.

"I can hardly wait to go exploring there," said Paul,
pointing, "and I believe it's all our land, right up to the
edge of the bush."

"And look, Paul," I cried with high excitement, "there are
four horses."

"Three of them are just plow and cart horses, by the look
of them," Paul noted, "but the bay pony looks as if he'd be
fine for riding."

That afternoon we had to help milk the cows and feed
the pigs. Dad had arranged for a hired man to come up
that day, but there was far too much for one man to do,
and we all pitched in. The farm work soon fell into a routine.

To my great disappointment, the bay pony proved a
bad-tempered creature with an ugly, jerky gait. We all
rode him to do necessary tasks, like rounding up the cows,
but he fell far short of my long-dreamed-of pony.

Meanwhile, Dad, who had no intention of being a farmer
for long, searched hard to find a buyer. In case that took

time, he began to sell off most of the milking cows and re-
place them with young beef cattle, which needed only
grazing. For that purpose we went to a stock sale that was
taking place nearby. I heard what happened later.

Up for sale was a sleek, slender black pony, half racehorse, with velvet eyes and a long, flowing mane and tail.

"I'm thinking of buying her for a child. Is she gentle?" my
father asked the owner.

"Gentle as a lamb to women and children," said the
farmer of this sleek black mare, "but I'll level with you. I'm
getting rid of her because she's vicious to most men. Some
brute must have mistreated her."

It did not seem possible. She rubbed her head against my
father's sleeve—but then he always had a way with animals.
When he took her for a trial ride, he seemed as if he were
floating on air, and she had perfect manners.

"If the price is right, I'll take her."

He bought her and came riding up on her to our farmhouse. "Alice," he called to Mother. "Come here a minute."

Catching a glimpse of the pony, I came out of the house
like a shot, but then I held back when I saw that my parents
wanted to talk alone. My heart raced. Could she be for me?

"Eve," Dad called, "come and meet your pony."

"Oh, Dad! Mother! She's beautiful! How perfect!" How
could I give them the thanks that were in my heart? She
was the pony of my dreams.

"We'll see if she'll let us ride her double-banked to the
auction, where I have to pick up the car," Dad said after I
had hugged them both in my happiness. "Then you can
bring her home alone and get acquainted. I bought the saddle and bridle with her, so the whole outfit is all yours."

She permitted us to "double-bank" on her, though I

hated to have her submit to this indignity, even for a short trip. She was made for prancing and racing, as anyone could see, but we went slowly while Dad told me all about her.

At last I rode back on her alone, having waved good-bye to Dad. When we reached a lonely stretch, I took her to the side of the road and dismounted. She nuzzled my hair.

"What shall I call you, beautiful? What's your name?"

She whinnied gently, as if trying to tell me.

"Peggy, shall I call you Peggy?"

She responded to my fondling of her neck with another rub of her nose against me. She seemed to approve of her name. It was one I had long used for my dream horse.

Very gently I tightened the girth and fondled her. "Now we're going to really ride together, Peggy," I said. She stood perfectly still while I mounted. I started her at a walk. She stepped proudly, picking up her feet smartly. Then I gave a flip of the reins, and she started ambling, in a smooth motion. I made a clicking sound in my cheek, gave another flick of the reins, and off she went at a swift, effortless trot, to which I posted. Oh, this was heaven!

We had come to a long, straight stretch of the road.

"Come, Peggy, let's go," I cried, flipping the reins and leaning forward. Catching my signal like a perfect dancing partner, Peggy leaped into a fast, eager canter, enjoying herself. I could feel the power in her strong shoulder muscles as she shot forward into a full gallop with the smooth, even strength of a bird's wing stroke. "Peggy, Pegasus, the winged horse," I murmured. That was who she was. I had named her well, I thought, as I suddenly recalled the Greek story; she was the myth-horse come to life again. "Peggy, Pegasus," I whispered again. I was leaning forward, gripping with my knees, the wind whipping my face and hair and Peggy's mane as the side of the road whizzed by us.

"Steady, Peggy! Steady!" I reined her in very gently and calmed her, for she wanted to keep racing up the hill ahead. I did not want to arrive at the farm with her overheated. She dropped back at my bidding to a canter, a trot, an amble, and then an eager walk, up and down the sharp rise and along the flat to the farm gate. Paul was waiting for me there and opened and closed the gate.

||≡||≡||≡||≡||≡||≡||≡||≡||≡||≡||≡||≡||≡||≡||≡||≡||≡||≡||≡|||

"Oh, you lucky one!" he said.

"Do you want to ride her?" I asked.

"Tomorrow, Eve," he said. "She's all yours today."

I was glad he understood how possessive I felt this first day. I unsaddled and unbridled her and rubbed her down till she was dry, then gave her some chaff and oats and let her take a light drink. After that I slipped a lead on her and took her down the field to introduce her to the other horses. The bay tried to bite her, but soon she became a member of the group. I slipped off the lead, and she started to crop the grass.

Halfway back to the house, just to test her, I called, holding out my hand in which I had hidden some oats, "Peggy! Peggy!" She looked up and came at a walk; then kicking up her heels, she came at a fast clip to me. She ate the oats ever so gently, so that only her lips touched my hand.

"Peggy," I murmured, "I can hardly wait to show you to Pita Tawa. You're much better than Sheila." I suppose it was mean—and foolish, too—but I did want to make him admit Peggy's superiority.

Paul was not horse-crazy as I was. The car was his great love. He would give it the same care I gave to Peggy. He and Dad spent hours on the Chevy, and already he could drive it around the farm—though not on the road, since he was too young.

That night, long after I had gone to bed, I could not sleep for happiness. I turned on my bedroom lamp, found an old notebook and pencil, and wrote a poem to celebrate. The first line was, "My fingers in my sweating pony's mane!"

The next day after breakfast, I had Peggy saddled and ready to ride—because I wanted to, but also because one

of our cows had made an escape through a break in our
boundary fence. Dad had gone down to mend the wires,
and I had volunteered to bring back the runaway, glad of
such an excellent excuse for a morning ride.

The cow was making her way up a hill directly in back of
our property, or at least in back of the part that was fenced,
for we were still rather vague about the boundary line. It
was a hill covered with thick bracken and ti trees; and on
its slope, in a small gully green with tree ferns, bubbled a
spring that was the source of the little stream running
through our farm.

I should have remembered to be careful in this place.
Only the day before, just before Dad had ridden up on my
pony, Paul had come in from an exploring trip over this
hill. It was the area he had planned to investigate when
we first saw it from our "little mountain" behind the house.
There was something about the shape of it that had stirred
his curiosity even at the first glance, though I, with my
attention on the four horses we had acquired with the farm,
had not noticed.

"Eve," he had called, excitement in his voice, "guess
what! I think we have an old Maori fort on or just behind
our farm! It's the hill where our stream starts up. Under
the scrub I could see the layout of the fosses and earth-
works, just like those at the model fortified village out at
Whaka."

The village at Whaka had been reconstructed to show
tourists what old Maori life was like. On our hill there
would be only the faintest remains of such a fort.

"Oh, Paul!" I exclaimed. "Can we take shovels and
spades and sort of clear it off and see if we can dig up any
ornaments or weapons?"

"We should probably tell Dad or Mother first," said Paul.

‖≣‖≣‖≣‖≣‖≣‖≣‖≣‖≣‖≣‖≣‖≣‖≣‖≣‖≣‖≣‖≣‖≣‖≣‖≣‖

"I think as a first step they'd burn off the brush when the wind was just right."

"Let's keep it our secret for a little while, until I can go and explore it with you," I begged. I was in the midst of doing the breakfast dishes at the moment. We knew it could be an important find. Dad had told us that this whole region was a favored one in Maori times, and the Arawa tribe of the lake sometimes had to fight off other tribes. This might be an outlying village fort, but more likely it was a temporary fort made during the wars between whites and Maoris.

Paul agreed that we would keep the fort a secret until I was able to look it over with him. But the arrival of Peggy in my life, just shortly afterward on this same morning, had put the old fort completely out of my mind.

Now, as I rode Peggy through the high scrub, I was intent only on recovering our stray cow. That miserable, stubborn beast kept doubling back, keeping us in the wretched scrub. The bushes scratched the pony's flanks and my bare legs, for I was wearing knee-length culottes. In the excitement of pursuit I never once thought about Paul's discovery.

Suddenly Peggy's feet shot from under her. I felt myself flying through the air over her head. I landed on the bank, and her hindquarters disappeared deep down in the darkness of a pit. Before I could move, she had plunged with her forefeet up on the bank out of the cramping hole into which they had slid at first, so that I found myself suddenly between her front legs, pinned there by my clothes under her hoofs. I lay helpless, looking up into the pony's terrified eyes as she gathered herself to plunge again. Had she done so, I would quite likely have been killed.

"Whoa, Peggy, whoa, Peggy. It's all right, Peggy," I said

‖≡‖

soothingly. Yet even as I was saying this, another part of my mind was racing: "I'm going to die now. I'll never grow up after all. I wonder what happens when you're dead, really."

But at the same time I kept my eyes fixed on Peggy and said, over and over, "Whoa, Peggy, whoa, Peggy. It's all right, Peggy." She responded to my voice. The terror started to pass out of her eyes. Still, she trembled all over. I kept on talking gently and soothingly to her as I eased up first one of her hoofs just a little and then the other. Little by little, I extricated myself, while she continued to obey me by standing still and throwing her weight slightly from one foot to the other at my easing. It was a strange upright posture that she had to keep. Not till I was clear and commanded her did she shift her feet.

I took the reins near her head, pulling them up from the darkness. Then, moving to one side, I encouraged her with them. "Up, Peggy, up, Peggy," I urged, putting pressure on my pull of the reins. She knew what I wanted; she wanted it, too. She gathered the splendid power of her thighs and haunches for a great, leaping plunge, and with me pulling hard on her bridle reins, she struggled out of that confining pit.

We bothered no further about the cow. Dad, I knew, would bring her in later. I just fondled Peggy over and over until she calmed down and stopped shivering, and by this time I felt capable of mounting. We picked our way carefully home, a shocked and subdued pair.

As I rode, I thought about many things. "If you hadn't loved me, Peggy," I said with a little shiver, "I don't believe I'd be here right now."

We were pampered, both Peggy and I, when we reached

║≡║

home and I told our tale. Later, we all made a thorough exploration of Paul's fort. We made a diagram and a map, with Dad doing most of it, and we sent it and some photographs to the Auckland museum. Our finds included an adze, or axe, and a *tiki*, or neck ornament, both made out of the hard New Zealand greenstone, a form of jade. Since the museum had many similar specimens, we were allowed to keep ours.

CHAPTER FIFTEEN

The Wild Ride

Peggy became the center of my life that summer. I spent hours grooming and training her and taking long, dreamy rides.

Mother and I often rode together, and during these rides I learned about her strict Presbyterian upbringing and the pranks she and her four sisters played on one another in their rivalry—and how they spoiled their young brother. She told me of our large clan of Scottish relatives in Dunedin, where she hoped to take me one day.

I learned, too, of some of Mother's own hair-raising experiences the year she was doing mission work before she and Dad were married. On those rides I also shared with Mother some of my poems and daydreams.

Sometimes when Paul was not off with the two boys of his own age who lived on the farm across the road from us, we spent time together.

"Let's gather blackberries today, Eve," he suggested one morning. "There's a grand place down the valley, this side of our clump of the bush."

"You take the bay, and I'll ride Peggy," I said.

We got pails for the berries, saddled the horses, and

started. Before long we were in the blackberry valley. These bushes grow gigantic in the moist New Zealand climate and bear fruit as large and sweetly luscious as the best cultivated berries in the United States.

"Dad will have to get these chopped out soon," said Paul. Blackberries are a pest on farmlands, and it was against the law to leave them growing.

"He'll have to get the ragwort cut out here, too," I said. It was perfuming the valley with its pungent odor and painting the hillside a vivid yellow. "Too bad it poisons stock. It looks so pretty."

"We can pick enough berries today to make jam and jelly and bottled fruit to last the whole year," exulted Paul. He was a conscientious picker. He would fill his pails before he settled down to eat his fill of the delicious fruit. I was the other type. I would always have to sample one here and one there, for each bush and each location on a bush seemed to bear fruit of a delicately different flavor. They were never so good as now, with the warm sunshine caught in them, or the coolness from the shade of a low branch close to the earth.

"You know, Paul," I confided as we picked, "I think I want to become a farmer. It's the life I like—tending live, growing things."

"Like chopping down blackberries and ragwort," teased Paul.

"Oh, partly it's the beauty," I said seriously, "sharing in the different moods of the day and the night and the seasons."

"It's terribly hard work," said Paul.

"I know, but I don't really mind that."

"What you like, you dreamy one," said Paul, "is not

having to keep to a clock and calendar too strictly. Just to drift along on the rhythm of the seasons and meet needs as they turn up."

He was right, this shrewd brother of mine. But it was more, too. I laughed and did not try to explain further. It was the freedom of not being directly under any boss, and it was Peggy, and churning our own golden fresh butter. It was also the smell of the earth and the cowshed; the vigor of the young calves and pigs as I fed them skimmed milk; the sound of a *tui* singing from one of our fence posts in the morning; the rabbits popping out in the evening to poach our pasture grass. I breathed deep, loving the sense of being alive.

Before the school vacation ended, our parents felt they had to return to the store. It was agreed that the hired man, Paul, and I would manage the farm until a buyer was found. This life was doing wonders for Paul, who was getting really husky. Mother managed to persuade a friend, whom we called Aunt Ada, though she was actually not related, to come and housekeep for us as a change from her city life in Auckland.

When the vacation ended, Paul and I went to the tiny part-time local school. One teacher looked after two schools, many miles apart, each for just half the week.

Sometimes we took our ponies, but more often we did not. The boys on the farm across the road, Mike and Saunders, could rarely get the use of a horse, so we often walked together. The road through the bush always felt lonely. It was easy to get lost in the bush, but we did sometimes take short cuts on paths we knew.

Our teacher was a retired, middle-aged British army officer who had a degree from an English university. We tried no nonsense with Major Burdock and struggled hard to meet his high demands. He drilled his assorted pupils into a semblance of military precision—how funny we must have looked!

In school he kept us all at work by getting older pupils to help teach the younger ones. This I loved to do.

"You know, Paul," I admitted one day, "I think I might sooner be a teacher than a farmer."

"I'd hate to be a teacher," was Paul's response.

Mother and Dad came up to the farm when they could, and always on Sunday. They had a telephone installed in order to keep in touch.

Sometimes I rode the seven miles down to the store for some errand by myself. I loved to do this, and so did Peggy. Each time I watched hopefully for Pita Tawa, for I had not forgotten how much I wanted to show him my pony. But for a long time it did not happen; possibly he was away visiting in another district.

There was a problem place on our route at about the halfway point. It was the turnoff onto an old, long-disused road over some steep hills and gullies. Repeatedly at this point I had to curb Peggy hard since, for some reason I did not understand, she always wanted to go up it.

One day on my way from the store back to the farm I was daydreaming as we approached the turnoff that charmed her so.

Suddenly she had the bit in her teeth and began racing at full gallop up this wild, broken road. I was powerless to control her, though I pulled on the reins with all my might. I was a strong girl, but my power was nothing compared to that of a determined Peggy. All I could do was try to stay in the saddle. I leaned forward and grabbed the

nape of her mane, as well as the saddle, and tightened rein.

Peggy began to soar over obstacles in her way and across chasms in the road. I had never jumped before, but I had watched Mabel do it, so I tried to remain "part of the horse," as she had explained the art to me.

How I kept in the saddle I do not know, nor how, sure-footed though she was, Peggy kept from tumbling on some of her wild jumps. This was rugged country, mainly burned-over second growth of bush and scrub. On and on she bolted, with no letup at all in her terrifying speed, no sign of wearying in her strong muscles. She seemed deaf to my tearful pleadings—a Peggy I had not known before.

Then, quite suddenly, she pulled herself down to a trot. There before us lay what must have been an old farm, for several years deserted. It had the forlorn skeletons of a farmhouse and outbuildings, and young trees were beginning to grow through several of them where the roofs had given way. Peggy looked around and then, in front of one of the buildings, she stopped completely.

I was still trembling with fear, but I realized her bolt was over. She had become quiet and controllable once more. Why had she wanted to come to this forlorn spot? Then I suspected that I understood.

"Peggy, Peggy," I said, fondling her, "I just bet, when you were a tiny filly, you lived here."

I dismounted, stiff and bruised, and sat down on the edge of the sun- and wind-warped verandah.

"Well now," I said, "since you've told me all about it, how about our going back?"

The return trip was going to be difficult. Would Peggy, now that she was calm, be able to negotiate those rugged gullies, I wondered. I certainly did not want to have to jump them again with her, and it might be hard to find ways to climb down and up them.

It was high time to be starting, however. Dad had phoned Aunt Ada when I left the store, saying when to expect me home at the farm. They always checked in that way in case I should have some mishap. I knew Dad or Mother would be coming pretty soon in the car or on a borrowed horse. They would be certain to notice those telltale, deeply dug tracks where Peggy had left the main road. Yes, I could expect a rescue party, so we had better start to meet it.

I mounted, and Peggy proceeded sweetly on the return trip. We had negotiated the first two gullies, after a time of scouting their banks, when I saw a horse and rider approaching over the farthest ridge in sight. It was Dad on a borrowed horse, and as he came close enough for me to recognize him, a wave of relief swept over me.

He hallooed as soon as he could. "You all right?"

"We're both all right," I called back.

He rode up beside me, and leaned over to stroke Peggy's lather-flecked flank.

"Mother and I guessed this little piece of black mischief might have bolted with you at her favorite corner. She must remember this road," he said.

"Who lived in the old farm up there, Dad?" I asked.

"It was a redheaded bachelor farmer called Patrick Casey, as I recall; mostly he dealt in Rotorua and then, when the Marvin store started up opposite us, he went there. I think he was 'agin' us."

"Do you know anything much about him?" I asked.

"Not really, but he was a friend of the O'Days. Old Mr.

||≡||≡||≡||≡||≡||≡||≡||≡||≡||≡||≡||≡||≡||≡||≡||≡||≡||≡||≡||≡||≡|||

O'Day is working on the road a little beyond the point where Peggy bolted, so you can ask him as you pass on the way up to the farm—unless you want to come back and spend the night with Mother and me."

Our horses were standing side by side. I reached out my hand and squeezed his. "I'd love to, Dad," I said. "But I really feel fine now that you're here, and I think I should go on and do my share of the milking."

"What a responsible, grown-up daughter you are getting to be these days!" Dad laughed. "Yes, you're right, and if you really feel well enough after your rough ride, it would be better to push on to the farm."

Now that Dad was with me, it was no trick at all to find a way back. He had a way of making all difficulties melt away. I enjoyed this visit alone with him. I missed his companionship now that we were living on the farm. All too soon, we came to the main road.

"Well, here's where I leave you, Eve. Ride well, and good luck!"

With those cheery words, he turned his horse and headed back toward the store.

I trotted Peggy to the spot, about a mile away, where Sandy O'Day was at work. The wizened little Irishman was paid by the government Public Works Department to tend and repair the roads of the area.

"Good afternoon, Mr. O'Day," I said as I approached him.

He stopped work and leaned on his shovel. He loved a chance to do this. He hated the new motor traffic that whizzed by and splashed mud on him, never stopping to gossip.

"Well now, Miss Eve," he said, wheezing through his

nose—he suffered badly from asthma and talked in a very nasal, high-pitched voice in a thoroughly Irish brogue— "it's a long toime since I've seen you, and we're amissin' you in Tahitahi these days."

The O'Days lived almost next door to our store, by the bridge over the river. Their old cottage had a hedge of sweet-smelling honeysuckle mixed with periwinkles. Two tall cabbage trees (the New Zealand "palm lily tree," with heads of swordlike leaves) stood outside their cluttered verandah.

"Mr. O'Day," I said, "can you tell me anything about Patrick Casey? Dad says he had a farm up that old road."

"Sure can, Miss Eve," he said, rolling himself a cigarette. He loved to tell a story as much as Pita did.

"Patrick Casey was a grand man, he wer; but he would get drunk often, and when he'd had the bottle, he sure wer a devil! I shouldn't say that word to you, but he wer that sure enough.

"He wer a great judge of horseflesh, though, right that he wer! I remember he had one great black stallion there that made a name for hisself, with us sinners as goes to racetracks." This was a sly dig at my parents, who disapproved of betting.

"What was the stallion's name?" I asked eagerly, thinking of Pita's story.

Mr. O'Day looked at me sharply out of his small, screwed-up eyes. "What for you be asking that, Miss Eve?" He scratched his head. "I'm kind of forgetting, but I think it wer Black Kerry. Yes, that wer it, Black Kerry."

"Black Keri," I said aloud, giving it the Maori pronunciation as Pita had done.

"Yes, Black Kerry. He had several black mares, too, come

to think of it. He'd have fancied that one of yours, now. Said he liked black horses because they matched his moods and because they looked so good in Ireland in his home place, 'gainst the green of the grass an' the shamrocks. He raised a lot of young colts. That ain't one of 'em by any chance?" He was looking harder at Peggy. "Bless me old heart if it don't look like one of 'em Casey horses, now I come to look real close!"

If I had not already heard Pita's story, I should have guessed that the old man was making all this up just to please me. But Black Kerry must surely be Pita's Black Keri. Here was Peggy's background at last, and I could not have hoped for a more romantic one.

"Sired by the great racehorse Black Kerry," I told myself, "on the stud farm of Patrick Casey." Yes, it sounded great. And it put me one up on Pita, who had owned her father only after he was dead.

But I had to put one more test upon Mr. O'Day. "How did he treat his horses?" If he were making this tale up for me, I would catch him here. "Did he break them in himself?"

"When he wer sober, he wer a great horse trainer and breaker," replied Mr. O'Day, "but sometimes, when he'd come back from Rotorua—he allers dealt there so he could do a good booze—he wer awful mean. He wer a black devil at them times, and pity the poor pony he wer handlin'! He'd go kinda mad!"

"Thank you! Thank you very much, Mr. O'Day," I said. "Yes, I think this may very well be one of his ponies." Then I added, "Why did Mr. Casey give up his farm and go away?"

"Ah! That wer quite a tale!" said Mr. O'Day, getting ready to roll another cigarette.

"I'll have to hear it some other day," I replied, looking at the western sun. "I've got to get home to help with the milking."

"Good lass!" said Mr. O'Day. "Well, the story will keep. But to put it brief, he met a rich widow on a drinking bout, and he went off and married her an' got set for life, he did. But there's more to it."

"I bet there is," I told him. "I'll ask about it someday. Greetings to Mrs. O'Day, and thanks so much for telling me about the Casey farm." I gave him a wave as I rode off.

Paul and Aunt Ada and even the hired man were relieved to see me arrive and listened to my tale of Peggy's ancestry.

"Peggy Kerry King," exclaimed Paul. "Quite a name!"

"She's Irish like I am," said Aunt Ada with a laugh.

Not long after that, on another trip down to the store, I met Pita. We were hitching Peggy and Sheila to the same railing, in front of our store.

"*Pai kori!*" he said, the Maori expression meaning "By golly!" as his eyes roved over the fine points of my pony. "That a great mare, that! Belong you, Eve?"

"Yes, Pita, she's all mine."

Pita extended his hand and ran sensitive fingers along her neck and down her shoulders. Peggy turned her head to him and rubbed her nose against his shirt.

"She likes you, Pita," I said.

"*Pai kori!* She great horse—racehorse—like Black Keri!" he said softly. "Eve, you got much better pony than Pita Tawa!"

"Thank you, Pita, thank you! But Sheila's a fine mare, too," I replied. Right then, I completely forgave him. All the old resentment left me.

"I've missed seeing you for so long, Pita," I told him.

CHAPTER SIXTEEN

Farewell

Winter began on the farm. We still went to school with bare legs and sandals. Often on clear, crisp mornings, when the porous earth along the cuttings had thrust up crusts of small ice needles like inverted fur coats of frost, we would slip off our sandals and crush the needles beneath our tough, bare feet. In the mornings Paul would shout, "Let's see how thick the ice is on the horse trough." This was his thermometer. He would hold up the glittering, diamond-clear sheets in the sunshine.

It was then, in wintry June, that Dad and Mother found a purchaser for our farm. They figured they had made no profit but had recovered what they had put into it.

"The farm has brought good things to our family," said Mother. It had indeed.

We returned to our store home in Tahitahi. It was fun to be back, but we would not get to stay long.

The wholesale merchant who had helped to finance our parents' store was building a series of chain stores through the whole province; ours was one of many country stores deeply in his debt. He now suddenly refused to renew loans to their owners, demanding immediate cash payments. Most of the storekeepers could not raise enough money to pay him, so they were compelled to sell to him on his terms.

Dad was caught in the trap, and there was nothing he could do. Almost all the Maori families, most of the farmers, and a few of the mill people owed him money—much of it sure to be repaid in time. But he could not suddenly collect it without ruining other lives, which was something he would not do. The blow fell early in the spring.

"Do you want me to sell or mortgage the properties you put in my name, Martin?" asked Mother. "They might raise enough."

"No, Alice, but thank you so much for offering. Those properties are a family lifeline. It's better to let the business go. My stubbornness has brought this on us," Dad replied, grief in his voice.

"Don't ever say that, or even think it," Mother replied. "You did what you felt you had to do."

I loved Mother for saying this. In days to come she never once, by look or word, threw up to Dad the fact that she had foreseen and warned of this danger for a very long time. "Goodness, I could never be like that!" I thought.

Paul and I were stupefied with shock and sorrow. We wandered around our home and our yard, handling and bidding a good-bye to each precious object and fragrant plant. We wandered around the garden, toying with the breath-of-heaven, the lemon verbena, the primroses, the frisias just starting to bloom.

One evening, when we were sitting at the table over a rather hastily prepared evening meal, Ted came to see our parents.

"Will you have something with us?" Mother asked.

"No thank you, Mrs. King, but I'd like a cup of tea," Ted replied. "It's a bad time, I know, on account of the children, but there's a piece of business I must discuss at once."

"The children are in this with us," said Dad, "so you may speak in front of them."

"It's a matter I'll say no to at once if you'd prefer it that way," said this loyal friend. "I think you've probably guessed that Ruth and I are planning to get married—"

"We'll not ask you to say no to that," said Dad, laughing. His interruption released some of the pent-up tensions. Ted had been courting the pretty daughter of our rival storekeeper across the street. We were very happy about it.

"Have you asked her?" Mother inquired.

"Just now," Ted admitted, coloring a little. "This evening we're officially engaged, and we plan to marry almost immediately."

"Congratulations!" we chorused.

"But that isn't what I thought you might want to say no about," said Ted, with a return of his nervous look.

"Shall I say it for you?" asked Dad.

Ted laughed. "Well, here goes. I've been asked to manage this place when it becomes a chain store. I don't have to. I can get other work. I'll say no if you would prefer it."

"By all means accept the position," said Dad. "It's a nice start for you two as a young couple."

"We'll be glad to know there is some continuity for our old customers," said Mother. She looked across at Dad, and there was a wordless communication between them.

Then Dad said, "There's something else, Ted, we'll trust you with. We haven't been paid any 'good will' for the business, so we've told the firm's representative that as soon as we're ready, we'll build up another store on our property on the corner of the side road. It will be just a small cash store, since we don't want anything more to do with credit and debts. It should be built by the end of the year, and we'll need someone to run it or lease it. If you and Ruth would like to make a change at that time, you can plan on taking it over, and if you like, you can gradually buy it yourselves. The cottage on the terrace above it could be home."

Ted's face glowed with pleasure. "Oh, we'd love to have a business of our own—and in competition with Ruth's old man, eh?" He chuckled. "But you're right. Tahitahi is growing, and there's room for a cash store that specializes in certain lines. It would be a good life for us."

"Let it be a secret between the six of us," said Mother. "Ruth and Eve are two women who can keep a secret." I beamed at the compliment.

The next morning, as we were preparing to vacate our store home, who should come in the gate that led through the garden to the front door but Pita Tawa.

"There's that rogue coming to gloat over you!" said Mother to Dad. "You go out to him, Martin. I couldn't face him this morning."

Pita approached with his usual benign, bland face and shining eyes. Paul and I, who were looking out of the window by the front door, noticed that he was carrying in his hand, clutched along with the crossbar of his crutch, a bulging sack that looked like an old sugar sack full of crumpled paper.

"I wonder what he's carrying?" Paul said to me.

"Maybe he's been robbing the bank!" I murmured.

"*Aue*, Martini Kingi, it is sad news that we hear!" Pita said. "You have no store any more!"

"Yes," Dad replied to him, "we have had to sell. Oh,

well! I can do with a rest and an easier life, and so can my *wahine*." A *wahine* is Maori for "woman" or "wife."

Pita Tawa came closer to my father, and as Maoris do at times of deep sympathy or emotion, as when old friends meet or part, he touched his nose to my father's.

"All the Maori very sorry," he said. "You and your *wahine* and children our very good friend." He paused. Maoris always do things in a dramatic style. Then he drew himself up very straight and said, "We collect all money we can around here. Maybe not enough to keep that store but enough so you know the Maori love you well."

With a sweeping gesture he opened the sack and poured out on the porch by the front door, at my father's feet, such a pile of money as I had never seen before. There were one-pound notes and five-pound notes and ten- and twenty-pound notes, mostly very dirty and crumpled, as if they had been at the bottom of some old baskets hanging from smoky rafters for a long time—and they probably had. There were even a lot of tinkling half crowns and florins and shillings, but mainly there were notes.

I could tell how moved Dad was. Mother, watching from the window with us, had also seen and heard. She sobbed out loud. "And I called him a rogue, God forgive me!"

He was, though, but a nice rogue.

Dad took Pita's hand. "We have a saying," he said. " 'A friend in need is a friend indeed.' You have done for us all more than I can ever tell you, for you have cheered our hearts in this dark time and given us new hope and faith and courage. Please thank all the Maori friends who have contributed this magnificent gift. We are grateful with all our hearts. And thank you, Pita, especially, for I know that this is mainly your doing. God bless you." Then he repeated all that he had said in fluent Maori, in which it

was sure to be more expressive and vivid, for Dad knew that although Pita was proud that he could speak and understand English, he would catch all the shades and flavors of meaning even better in his own language.

Then the two of them fell to gathering up all this money and stuffing it back into the sack, partly because it had to be done, but mainly, I felt, because these two men wanted to ignore the fact that both of them had tears coursing down their faces.

"You know, Alice," Dad said as we sat at lunch later that day, "I just hate to mention this, and I hope that what has happened here in the store over the last few weeks hasn't given me a suspicious mind. But I can't keep from feeling anxious about this Pita Tawa gift. I hate to face it even myself, but it's a matter in which we must be very wise and discreet."

"What is it you fear, Martin?" Mother asked.

Paul and I both stopped short with pieces of bread half-way to our mouths. It was a strange statement to hear from our father, whom we had never before heard voice a suspicion of anyone.

"Alice," Dad said in a somewhat hesitant voice, "it is, as you know, a Maori custom to help generously like this in a crisis, particularly in the case of those who belong in any way to them—and of course we do. But it is not characteristic for them to let Pita Tawa, who isn't even a chief, bring the gift. I find it strange that no villagers were along, especially since they know he can't be trusted with money."

"I've been worried by the same thing, Martin, and I've hated to bring it up for fear it was my suspicious nature," Mother replied. "Where do you think he got it? It's Maori money all right. I can tell that from the way it is crumpled and smoke-soiled from their poorly chimneyed houses, and it smells of their tobacco."

"The families from whom it came probably all owed us money," said Dad, "much more than these 'donations.' In his mind, part Maori and part smart European in its working, Pita probably thought—if he *did* take the money— 'It belongs to Kingi anyway. I'll just take it to him.' He would feel perfectly justified in doing it—not that it would worry Pita if he didn't feel justified! He loves the excitement of playing the rogue."

To Paul and me this was a horrid thought. We had been so pleased and comforted by this "donation" of Maori money, and we really loved Pita Tawa.

But Pita, I thought, would be just the one to have observed where these little wads and bundles of money were hidden and to keep the knowledge stored for when it might be useful. I could see him visiting at house after house, as he loved to do, and keeping the conversation going until, like a magician, those quick, clever fingers could extract a little bundle of notes from this or that basket or kit bag sitting in a corner or tied to a rafter of the low-built Maori houses. Such houses were usually dark and often without windows.

If this was what had happened, it could be months till the losses were discovered. It would not be till an important wedding, or *tangi*, or something of the kind drew on the hidden family reserves.

"If you were sure of it, Martin, if you knew that Pita had just plain 'stolen' the money—let's face the word—what would you do?" Mother asked.

"That's partly what bothers me so," Dad said. "I'm not sure. In the first place, he may not really have 'stolen' it.

He may have shamed them into giving it, as he so well could. You know how the Maori will do almost anything to avoid or escape from a sense of shame."

"Would that explain everything?" Mother asked.

"I think it might," Dad replied. "If they were shamed into parting with it, they might well have felt like leaving Pita, a mere commoner, to bring the gift. I rather think that's what happened."

"Would they trust him to deliver it?" Mother asked. They seemed to have forgotten our presence at the table, and we were too absorbed by this problem to do anything other than listen quietly.

"How do we know," Dad replied, "that there were not half a dozen observers of the scene this morning? If a Maori wants to spy on anything, no *pakeha* is likely to find out that he is doing so." *Pakeha* is the Maori word for a white person.

Paul and I exchanged glances. It was exciting to think that our front-door scene had been observed by hidden Maoris. But it was sad to have such a beautiful experience turned into something rather ugly. And having personally forgiven Pita for my real or imaginary grievance, I could not bear to have my feelings about him mixed up again.

"On the other hand," Mother continued, "Pita has 'taken' us so many times. It would be exactly like him to play Robin Hood and steal the money for us now. He'd be forgiven by the Maoris—you know he would. He reminds them of the warring, raiding past that isn't so very far back and about which they love to tell their children: When the war canoes sneaked across Lake Rotorua. . . . They don't like the tameness of life today."

"I wouldn't bring in any white authority," Dad said firmly. "I couldn't do that. Even if he stole it, he did it as a gesture of love," he continued. "In his eyes it really was our money, whatever the white law may say."

"Oh, Dad," I exclaimed, "it was such a beautiful thing to have happen. I can't bear to think it's really stolen money."

"You'd have to find some way of giving it back," said Paul. "But how? I can't think of a way."

"Perhaps," said Dad, "if I can ever find out the truth, and it turns out to be that he helped himself to it on our behalf, I could get him to see the need to return it secretly, the way he took it."

Mother's rippling laugh rang out. "Oh, Martin!" she exclaimed. "Do you think Pita would ever put the money back? He'd say to himself, 'If Kingi is such a fool *pakeha* that he won't take his own money when I bring it to him, Pita Tawa is *not* a fool. He is a Maori!' And into his pocket, or his un-Maori savings account, it would go."

Mother was right. She knew people the way Dad knew Maori custom.

"We'll have to see about it," said Dad. "The hard thing is to live on the slidy top of a question mark."

But that was where we remained. The uncertainty of it hung over our heads, never quite forgotten through the months that followed, like a thundercloud that will not break.

That very afternoon we started the move across the road to the higher of the two cottages that Dad had built during the time we were at the farm. We took with us all of our treasures that the smaller cottage home would contain.

"Children," Dad remarked, "like trees, need their roots balled up during a shift and all the soil that is possible taken with them."

‖≡‖

"Soil is right," said Mother with a laugh. But she, too, was a hoarder and indulged us in this all she could, though it did not make her housekeeping easier.

We delighted in our cottage home. Dad was fascinated during this period by the idea of wide verandahs that joined with and almost became part of the garden. He had built the room that Paul and I shared with a partial partition for privacy, and with large glass panel doors that slid smoothly on ball bearings so that they would open the room almost completely to the wide verandah. He loved to see us sprawled there in the sun.

In addition to whatever regular work he was doing, Dad believed in always having a family project underway. That spring we made a tennis court and learned to play the game.

"Why go to all this trouble when we may so soon be leaving Tahitahi?" Mother questioned.

"Even if we leave, we'll be coming back often, and the court will be here for our pleasure," Dad replied. "If the children learn to play a good game of tennis now, they may enjoy playing all their lives—till they're eighty perhaps!" He allowed a good run-back area all around, laying it out according to a book he had bought, and he built a high netting fence so we would not have to chase balls far. It was a fine court, with a view of the lake, for it was part of the great lawn on the terrace between our cottage and the lodge. Guests at the lodge often joined us in play, and so did some school friends. From the first, Paul was the star, thanks to his good coordination and tiger-quick reactions.

"Where am I going to high school?" I asked several

||≡||≡||≡||≡||≡||≡||≡||≡||≡||≡||≡||≡||≡||≡||≡||≡||≡||≡||≡||≡||≡||≡||≡||≡||≡|||

times as the school year continued to slip by. I would soon graduate from Tahitahi school.

"We're thinking about it," was the only answer I received for a long time. But finally, one November day, Paul and I were called in to a family conference.

"We can answer your question, now, Eve," Dad said. "The new small store I have been building is, as you know, complete, and today Ted and Ruth have leased it and the lower cottage. They plan to buy them both. As soon as you two complete the school year, we'll rent this cottage and be ready for a journey."

"Oh, where to?" asked Paul, a shade of anxiety in his voice.

"You know," Dad continued, "how Mother has seen almost nothing of her relatives for years. We're planning to go to Auckland by train and then take a steamer and go by sea all the way to Dunedin on the South Island. You, Eve, will have your first year of high school at Girls High School, Dunedin. Paul, you'll benefit by a city school for a year, too."

"Then where?" I asked.

"Well, after that," said Dad, "unless we all want to stay in Dunedin—and I don't think we will—we'll probably come back to the North Island where nearly all the Maoris live, and we think we'll settle in Tauranga. There is need for medical mission work there, and that is what Mother and I would like to do for the rest of our lives."

"Dad," I exclaimed as this great package of news unrolled, "how great to make a real ocean voyage!"

"They have cable cars in Dunedin, don't they?" asked Paul.

I could tell Mother was watching our reactions. I put my arms around her neck.

"Mother, it's going to be fun meeting Grandma and getting to know our cousins," I said, "and I'm glad you're going home for a visit at last."

"Oh, Eve, I'm pleased you feel that way." She sighed, relief in her voice. "I was worrying in case my little savage of a daughter would dread going to a city school."

"I guess I can wear stockings and gloves and a hat for a year," I said. "But I'm sure Dad is right about our not wanting to stay there too long. After all, Paul and I are country bumpkins, you know, and I really think you and Dad are, too."

"You're probably right," she admitted. "But what I expected you to worry about most you haven't mentioned yet."

"Her beloved Peggy!" Paul put in with a mischievous grin.

"I've been thinking about it, though," I said, "and I'm pretty sure Mabel would look after her for me. Mabel said the other day she'd like to ride her in the show this year, and I said she could."

"Dad," said Paul, "if we live in Tauranga, could we go to the Mount for holidays?"

"Certainly we could," said Dad. "Meanwhile, you had both better work hard at school this last month so you'll be ready to show up those city children."

We both giggled. We knew how much it would be the other way around. But what would have worried us a year or so ago, when we felt we could never leave Tahitahi, we could now take in our stride.

"I can hardly wait," said Paul, "to get aboard that ship."

I was dreaming of that coastal voyage, too, but not the way Paul was. I was remembering that I would have the unpleasant task of explaining to Grandma that I no longer had the pearl brooch. But I kept this to myself, as I had all along.

News that we were leaving at the end of the year spread like flames. No doubt Paul and I had lit the match by boasting at school of our coming voyage. Old friends threw parties for us. Since we no longer owned the store and had suffered adversity, our popularity had strangely increased.

"I think I'm the one who'll miss you the most," said Uncle David sadly on one of our last fishing trips with him.

"Oh, we'll be back, Uncle David, and we'll write to you often."

The school board honored their retiring president, who had served ever since it first came into being, with a wooden wall plaque, duly inscribed—a treasure Dad was proud of. Then a message came to Dad and Mother that a *hui*, a large gathering and feast in honor of our family, was to be held in the great meeting house of Tahitahi Maori village on the next Saturday.

Our parents were deeply troubled by this development. How would they act, or reply to speeches, when they were not sure whether they had received an all-important gift of money or were holding stolen loot? The Pita Tawa situation remained a riddle.

Saturday, the time of the *hui*, came. We walked sedately, decked out in our best clothes, down the dusty road beyond the butter factory and the railway line to the path that led into the *pa*, the Maori village, and up to the impressive old meeting house. It stood in an open space within a wide coil of the river; this space was the *marae*, or meeting area of the village. Maoris from all around, and from the smaller villages by this part of the lake, had assembled.

Dad had prepared Paul and me for what was now about to happen.

Where the path led off from the public road, a Maori man suddenly sprang out at us, shouting and gesticulating wildly and making the fierce faces of the war dance as he brandished a spear. He was clad in the traditional plaited flax waist mat and cloak. My father continued his approach, and we followed him, ignoring the "challenger."

Then the warrior laid his spear at my father's feet. Lining the path to the meeting house were the women of the village, especially the old *wahines,* to do us honor. They waved green branches and fronds or mats as they cried loud greetings and made dance movements to old welcoming chants. A crowd of men, women, and children pressed forward behind them, joining in the noisy demonstration.

All were in their finest clothes, some with bright cloth garments and gay kerchiefs, more with some form of the old flax clothing, often tops over modern trousers or dresses. This was a first-class *hui* that was being given for us. We felt grateful and honored.

We stopped just in front of the meeting house, facing a welcoming group that met us there. Then began a great wailing as noses were touched and tears streamed. Paul and I had our noses duly rubbed, too. We were glad when this part of the ceremony was over and we were ushered through the one door into the impressive dimness of the spacious interior of the house. On the floor were finely plaited mats on which the Maoris would sit; for us chairs were provided. The one small window in the front gave enough light for us to see the chiefs, each seating himself in his correct place. My father was escorted to a position on the right-hand side reserved for the guest of honor. His *wahine* and children were seated beside him. Everyone packed in somewhere, sitting cross-legged or with knees drawn up to their faces.

I took in the beautiful rush-work of the walls and the rafter patterning in black and red and white dyes that made this so impressive. Everywhere was the strong smell of Maori tobacco and aging flax.

Soon the head chief stood to make an oration, an address of honor and welcome and farewell. My knowledge of Maori enabled me to catch words that sent relief and joy surging through me—and I knew Dad and Mother must have felt the same.

"We have grieved," the orator said, "that at the time we made the small gift from our hearts, when the great misfortune struck upon your door, there was no opportunity to make a formal presentation in a Maori manner. It was a matter of quick action, like stemming the sudden assault of a foe. We are glad that now we may honor you, Martini Kingi, and your *wahine* and your boy and girl, who have been such good friends to all the Maori people of this district for these many years; that we may recognize you in a style more appropriate to your great respect for Maori ways. We would thank, too, the good God who has put into your hearts so much concern for the welfare of the Maori people.

"Today we would like to ask you, when you reply to this talk, to lead us in a prayer that God may bless you on your journeys, wherever you may go, and that He may also bless us here in our lives in Tahitahi, in these difficult days when we, too, make a journey into new strange ways of living."

Dad's reply was, I am sure, as eloquent as the chief's, and

they all responded to his prayer at the end with fervent amens. Then, spontaneously, the people broke into some of their favorite hymns, many of them learned in our parents' old school, beautifully harmonized by the rich, strong voices.

After more ceremonial speeches, we were taken outside to where the *wahines* had prepared a huge and delicious feast. We sat on clean flax mats. Other mats acted as dishes for our hosts, but our portions were brought on plates. The food was mainly pork, chicken, and lake trout, with *kumara* and greens, cooked by slow steaming in an earth oven. We knew that in the morning a fire had been made in the great pit that was the oven. On the fire were laid stones, which gradually became very hot. Then moist leaves and mats were laid on the stones, and the food carefully placed on them. The dressed pig was put in whole, and the fish and other smaller things were arranged in flax kits or in leaves. More mats were laid over these to protect them well, and earth was piled over to shut in the steam. Slowly the whole meal had cooked to perfection.

Many amusing tales went around as our Maori friends recalled episodes in our parents' lives. They joked about the time my father had made the house that had become the mission school "walk along the road" to where he wanted it. In fact, it had been drawn by a team of bullocks. They recalled the adventure we children had on Mokoia Island, when Tawhia had built his signal fire, and many other stories that passed over Paul's and my head since they were in rapid Maori.

As a token of friendship, gifts were presented—and of course this meant more speeches and more replies. Mother looked charming with the dancing skirt they gave her, along with a pair of *poi* balls. The young women did a *poi* dance; then they came forward, took Mother's hand, and urged her to accompany them, which she did tolerably well and for which she was loudly applauded. The young men put on a war dance and presented Dad with an orator's staff "on which to lean as you do your preaching." There were warm handclasps as our Maori friends each said farewell in modern style. Not least among these was Pita Tawa, his eyes especially bright.

I was the last in the line of our family, for in the Maori order of honor my brother as a boy took precedence over me. As Pita clasped my hand, he slipped me a small package wrapped in brown paper. I sensed that this was between him and me and that he did not want me to open it there. I quickly put it into my shoulder bag.

At last we were on the main road back, with a group of young Maoris carrying our gifts. All four of us were weary but very happy.

As soon as we were alone I said, "So Pita did collect the money honestly, and it's all right."

"We must give thanks that the truth was made plain in time this afternoon," replied Mother fervently.

Dad laughed. "I shall never be sure, really, how that money was collected. But the Maoris have dealt with it in their own way, and no *pakeha* will ever know any more about it than we do now. I'm glad of that."

I excused myself as soon as I could and slipped away to my room. I knew, without opening that package, what would be in it. My fingers shook as I undid the brown wrapping. There it lay—my long-lost box. Within was the exquisite pearl brooch, none the worse for its adventures, whatever they had been. I felt like Dad. I was glad I did not have to know.

DATE DUE

JUN 24 '85			
DEC 30 '85			
FEB. 1 '7 1986			
FEB 1 5 '92			
GAYLORD			PRINTED IN U.S.A.